Poems

By

Robert Southey

The Echo Library 2006

Published by

The Echo Library

Echo Library
131 High St.
Teddington
Middlesex TW11 8HH

www.echo-library.com

Please report serious faults in the text to complaints@echo-library.com

ISBN 1-4068-2301-5

CONTENTS

THE VISION of THE MAID of ORLEANS.
    Book 1   01
    Book 2   12
    Book 3   23
The Rose   31
The Complaints of the Poor   35
Metrical Letter   37
BALLADS.
The Cross Roads.   39
    The Sailor who had served in the Slave Trade   43
    Jaspar   47
    Lord William   53
    A Ballad shewing how an old woman rode double and who rode before her   57
    The Surgeon's Warning   64
    The Victory   69
    Henry the Hermit   71
ENGLISH ECLOGUES.   73
    The Old Mansion House   74
    The Grandmother's Tale   79
    The Funeral   84
    The Sailor's Mother   86
    The Witch   91
    The Ruined Cottage   97

THE VISION OF THE MAID OF ORLEANS

THE FIRST BOOK

Orleans was hush'd in sleep. Stretch'd on her couch
The delegated Maiden lay: with toil
Exhausted and sore anguish, soon she closed
Her heavy eye-lids; not reposing then,
For busy Phantasy, in other scenes
Awakened. Whether that superior powers,
By wise permission, prompt the midnight dream,
Instructing so the passive [1] faculty;
Or that the soul, escaped its fleshly clog,
Flies free, and soars amid the invisible world,
And all things 'are' that [2] 'seem'.

           Along a moor,
Barren, and wide, and drear, and desolate,
She roam'd a wanderer thro' the cheerless night.
Far thro' the silence of the unbroken plain
The bittern's boom was heard, hoarse, heavy, deep,
It made most fitting music to the scene.
Black clouds, driven fast before the stormy wind,
Swept shadowing; thro' their broken folds the moon
Struggled sometimes with transitory ray,
And made the moving darkness visible.
And now arrived beside a fenny lake
She stands: amid its stagnate waters, hoarse
The long sedge rustled to the gales of night.
An age-worn bark receives the Maid, impell'd
By powers unseen; then did the moon display
Where thro' the crazy vessel's yawning side
The muddy wave oozed in: a female guides,
And spreads the sail before the wind, that moan'd
As melancholy mournful to her ear,
As ever by the dungeon'd wretch was heard
Howling at evening round the embattled towers
Of that hell-house [3] of France, ere yet sublime
The almighty people from their tyrant's hand
Dash'd down the iron rod.
                Intent the Maid
Gazed on the pilot's form, and as she gazed
Shiver'd, for wan her face was, and her eyes
Hollow, and her sunk cheeks were furrowed deep,
Channell'd by tears; a few grey locks hung down

Beneath her hood: then thro' the Maiden's veins
Chill crept the blood, for, as the night-breeze pass'd,
Lifting her tatter'd mantle, coil'd around
She saw a serpent gnawing at her heart.

The plumeless bat with short shrill note flits by,
And the night-raven's scream came fitfully,
Borne on the hollow blast. Eager the Maid
Look'd to the shore, and now upon the bank
Leaps, joyful to escape, yet trembling still
In recollection.

        There, a mouldering pile
Stretch'd its wide ruins, o'er the plain below
Casting a gloomy shade, save where the moon
Shone thro' its fretted windows: the dark Yew,
Withering with age, branched there its naked roots,
And there the melancholy Cypress rear'd
Its head; the earth was heav'd with many a mound,
And here and there a half-demolish'd tomb.

And now, amid the ruin's darkest shade,
The Virgin's eye beheld where pale blue flames
Rose wavering, now just gleaming from the earth,
And now in darkness drown'd. An aged man
Sat near, seated on what in long-past days
Had been some sculptur'd monument, now fallen
And half-obscured by moss, and gathered heaps
Of withered yew-leaves and earth-mouldering bones;
And shining in the ray was seen the track
Of slimy snail obscene. Composed his look,
His eye was large and rayless, and fix'd full
Upon the Maid; the blue flames on his face
Stream'd a pale light; his face was of the hue
Of death; his limbs were mantled in a shroud.

Then with a deep heart-terrifying voice,
Exclaim'd the Spectre, "Welcome to these realms,
These regions of DESPAIR! O thou whose steps
By GRIEF conducted to these sad abodes
Have pierced; welcome, welcome to this gloom
Eternal, to this everlasting night,
Where never morning darts the enlivening ray,
Where never shines the sun, but all is dark,
Dark as the bosom of their gloomy King."

So saying he arose, and by the hand
The Virgin seized with such a death-cold touch
As froze her very heart; and drawing on,
Her, to the abbey's inner ruin, led
Resistless. Thro' the broken roof the moon
Glimmer'd a scatter'd ray; the ivy twined
Round the dismantled column; imaged forms
Of Saints and warlike Chiefs, moss-canker'd now
And mutilate, lay strewn upon the ground,
With crumbled fragments, crucifixes fallen,
And rusted trophies; and amid the heap
Some monument's defaced legend spake
All human glory vain.

          The loud blast roar'd
Amid the pile; and from the tower the owl
Scream'd as the tempest shook her secret nest.
He, silent, led her on, and often paus'd,
And pointed, that her eye might contemplate
At leisure the drear scene.
          He dragged her on
Thro' a low iron door, down broken stairs;
Then a cold horror thro' the Maiden's frame
Crept, for she stood amid a vault, and saw,
By the sepulchral lamp's dim glaring light,
The fragments of the dead.
          "Look here!" he cried,
"Damsel, look here! survey this house of Death;
O soon to tenant it! soon to increase
These trophies of mortality! for hence
Is no return. Gaze here! behold this skull,
These eyeless sockets, and these unflesh'd jaws,
That with their ghastly grinning, seem to mock
Thy perishable charms; for thus thy cheek
Must moulder. Child of Grief! shrinks not thy soul,
Viewing these horrors? trembles not thy heart
At the dread thought, that here its life's-blood soon
Now warm in life and feeling, mingle soon
With the cold clod? a thought most horrible!
So only dreadful, for reality
Is none of suffering here; here all is peace;
No nerve will throb to anguish in the grave.
Dreadful it is to think of losing life;
But having lost, knowledge of loss is not,
Therefore no ill. Haste, Maiden, to repose;

Probe deep the seat of life."
                    So spake DESPAIR
The vaulted roof echoed his hollow voice,
And all again was silence. Quick her heart
Panted. He drew a dagger from his breast,
And cried again, "Haste Damsel to repose!
One blow, and rest for ever!" On the Fiend
Dark scowl'd the Virgin with indignant eye,
And dash'd the dagger down. He next his heart
Replaced the murderous steel, and drew the Maid
Along the downward vault.
                    The damp earth gave
A dim sound as they pass'd: the tainted air
Was cold, and heavy with unwholesome dews.
"Behold!" the fiend exclaim'd, "how gradual here
The fleshly burden of mortality
Moulders to clay!" then fixing his broad eye
Full on her face, he pointed where a corpse
Lay livid; she beheld with loathing look,
The spectacle abhorr'd by living man.

"Look here!" DESPAIR pursued, "this loathsome mass
Was once as lovely, and as full of life
As, Damsel! thou art now. Those deep-sunk eyes
Once beam'd the mild light of intelligence,
And where thou seest the pamper'd flesh-worm trail,
Once the white bosom heaved. She fondly thought
That at the hallowed altar, soon the Priest
Should bless her coming union, and the torch
Its joyful lustre o'er the hall of joy,
Cast on her nuptial evening: earth to earth
That Priest consign'd her, and the funeral lamp
Glares on her cold face; for her lover went
By glory lur'd to war, and perish'd there;
Nor she endur'd to live. Ha! fades thy cheek?
Dost thou then, Maiden, tremble at the tale?
Look here! behold the youthful paramour!
The self-devoted hero!"
                    Fearfully
The Maid look'd down, and saw the well known face
Of THEODORE! in thoughts unspeakable,
Convulsed with horror, o'er her face she clasp'd
Her cold damp hands: "Shrink not," the Phantom cried,
"Gaze on! for ever gaze!" more firm he grasp'd
Her quivering arm: "this lifeless mouldering clay,

As well thou know'st, was warm with all the glow
Of Youth and Love; this is the arm that cleaved
Salisbury's proud crest, now motionless in death,
Unable to protect the ravaged frame
From the foul Offspring of Mortality
That feed on heroes. Tho' long years were thine,
Yet never more would life reanimate
This murdered man; murdered by thee! for thou
Didst lead him to the battle from his home,
Else living there in peace to good old age:
In thy defence he died: strike deep! destroy
Remorse with Life."
    The Maid stood motionless,
And, wistless what she did, with trembling hand
Received the dagger. Starting then, she cried,
"Avaunt DESPAIR! Eternal Wisdom deals
Or peace to man, or misery, for his good
Alike design'd; and shall the Creature cry,
Why hast thou done this? and with impious pride
Destroy the life God gave?"
    The Fiend rejoin'd,
"And thou dost deem it impious to destroy
The life God gave? What, Maiden, is the lot
Assigned to mortal man? born but to drag,
Thro' life's long pilgrimage, the wearying load
Of being; care corroded at the heart;
Assail'd by all the numerous train of ills
That flesh inherits; till at length worn out,
This is his consummation!--think again!
What, Maiden, canst thou hope from lengthen'd life
But lengthen'd sorrow? If protracted long,
Till on the bed of death thy feeble limbs
Outstretch their languid length, oh think what thoughts,
What agonizing woes, in that dread hour,
Assail the sinking heart! slow beats the pulse,
Dim grows the eye, and clammy drops bedew
The shuddering frame; then in its mightiest force,
Mightiest in impotence, the love of life
Seizes the throbbing heart, the faltering lips
Pour out the impious prayer, that fain would change
The unchangeable's decree, surrounding friends
Sob round the sufferer, wet his cheek with tears,
And all he loved in life embitters death!

Such, Maiden, are the pangs that wait the hour

Of calmest dissolution! yet weak man
Dares, in his timid piety, to live;
And veiling Fear in Superstition's garb,
He calls her Resignation!
     Coward wretch!
Fond Coward! thus to make his Reason war
Against his Reason! Insect as he is,
This sport of Chance, this being of a day,
Whose whole existence the next cloud may blast,
Believes himself the care of heavenly powers,
That God regards Man, miserable Man,
And preaching thus of Power and Providence,
Will crush the reptile that may cross his path!

Fool that thou art! the Being that permits
Existence, 'gives' to man the worthless boon:
A goodly gift to those who, fortune-blest,
Bask in the sunshine of Prosperity,
And such do well to keep it. But to one
Sick at the heart with misery, and sore
With many a hard unmerited affliction,
It is a hair that chains to wretchedness
The slave who dares not burst it!
     Thinkest thou,
The parent, if his child should unrecall'd
Return and fall upon his neck, and cry,
Oh! the wide world is comfortless, and full
Of vacant joys and heart-consuming cares,
I can be only happy in my home
With thee--my friend!--my father! Thinkest thou,
That he would thrust him as an outcast forth?
Oh I he would clasp the truant to his heart,
And love the trespass."
     Whilst he spake, his eye
Dwelt on the Maiden's cheek, and read her soul
Struggling within. In trembling doubt she stood,
Even as the wretch, whose famish'd entrails crave
Supply, before him sees the poison'd food
In greedy horror.
     Yet not long the Maid
Debated, "Cease thy dangerous sophistry,
Eloquent tempter!" cried she. "Gloomy one!
What tho' affliction be my portion here,
Think'st thou I do not feel high thoughts of joy,
Of heart-ennobling joy, when I look back

Upon a life of duty well perform'd,
Then lift mine eyes to Heaven, and there in faith
Know my reward? I grant, were this life all,
Was there no morning to the tomb's long night,
If man did mingle with the senseless clod,
Himself as senseless, then wert thou indeed
A wise and friendly comforter! But, Fiend!
There is a morning to the tomb's long night,
A dawn of glory, a reward in Heaven,
He shall not gain who never merited.
If thou didst know the worth of one good deed
In life's last hour, thou would'st not bid me lose
The power to benefit; if I but save
A drowning fly, I shall not live in vain.
I have great duties, Fiend! me France expects,
Her heaven-doom'd Champion."
                "Maiden, thou hast done
Thy mission here," the unbaffled Fiend replied:
"The foes are fled from Orleans: thou, perchance
Exulting in the pride of victory,
Forgettest him who perish'd! yet albeit
Thy harden'd heart forget the gallant youth;
That hour allotted canst thou not escape,
That dreadful hour, when Contumely and Shame
Shall sojourn in thy dungeon. Wretched Maid!
Destined to drain the cup of bitterness,
Even to its dregs! England's inhuman Chiefs
Shall scoff thy sorrows, black thy spotless fame,
Wit-wanton it with lewd barbarity,
And force such burning blushes to the cheek
Of Virgin modesty, that thou shalt wish
The earth might cover thee! in that last hour,
When thy bruis'd breast shall heave beneath the chains
That link thee to the stake; when o'er thy form,
Exposed unmantled, the brute multitude
Shall gaze, and thou shalt hear the ribald taunt,
More painful than the circling flames that scorch
Each quivering member; wilt thou not in vain
Then wish my friendly aid? then wish thine ear
Had drank my words of comfort? that thy hand
Had grasp'd the dagger, and in death preserved
Insulted modesty?"
              Her glowing cheek
Blush'd crimson; her wide eye on vacancy
Was fix'd; her breath short panted. The cold Fiend,

Grasping her hand, exclaim'd, "too-timid Maid,
So long repugnant to the healing aid
My friendship proffers, now shalt thou behold
The allotted length of life."
					He stamp'd the earth,
And dragging a huge coffin as his car,
Two GOULS came on, of form more fearful-foul
Than ever palsied in her wildest dream
Hag-ridden Superstition. Then DESPAIR
Seiz'd on the Maid whose curdling blood stood still.
And placed her in the seat; and on they pass'd
Adown the deep descent. A meteor light
Shot from the Daemons, as they dragg'd along
The unwelcome load, and mark'd their brethren glut
On carcasses.
		Below the vault dilates
Its ample bulk. "Look here!"--DESPAIR addrest
The shuddering Virgin, "see the dome of DEATH!"
It was a spacious cavern, hewn amid
The entrails of the earth, as tho' to form
The grave of all mankind: no eye could reach,
Tho' gifted with the Eagle's ample ken,
Its distant bounds. There, thron'd in darkness, dwelt
The unseen POWER OF DEATH.
			Here stopt the GOULS,
Reaching the destin'd spot. The Fiend leapt out,
And from the coffin, as he led the Maid,
Exclaim'd, "Where never yet stood mortal man,
Thou standest: look around this boundless vault;
Observe the dole that Nature deals to man,
And learn to know thy friend."
			She not replied,
Observing where the Fates their several tasks
Plied ceaseless. "Mark how short the longest web
Allowed to man! he cried; observe how soon,
Twin'd round yon never-resting wheel, they change
Their snowy hue, darkening thro' many a shade,
Till Atropos relentless shuts the sheers!"

Too true he spake, for of the countless threads,
Drawn from the heap, as white as unsunn'd snow,
Or as the lovely lilly of the vale,
Was never one beyond the little span
Of infancy untainted: few there were
But lightly tinged; more of deep crimson hue,

Or deeper sable [4] died. Two Genii stood,
Still as the web of Being was drawn forth,
Sprinkling their powerful drops. From ebon urn,
The one unsparing dash'd the bitter wave
Of woe; and as he dash'd, his dark-brown brow
Relax'd to a hard smile. The milder form
Shed less profusely there his lesser store;
Sometimes with tears increasing the scant boon,
Mourning the lot of man; and happy he
Who on his thread those precious drops receives;
If it be happiness to have the pulse
Throb fast with pity, and in such a world
Of wretchedness, the generous heart that aches
With anguish at the sight of human woe.

To her the Fiend, well hoping now success,
"This is thy thread! observe how short the span,
And see how copious yonder Genius pours
The bitter stream of woe." The Maiden saw
Fearless. "Now gaze!" the tempter Fiend exclaim'd,
And placed again the poniard in her hand,
For SUPERSTITION, with sulphureal torch
Stalk'd to the loom. "This, Damsel, is thy fate!
The hour draws on--now drench the dagger deep!
Now rush to happier worlds!"
              The Maid replied,
"Or to prevent or change the will of Heaven,
Impious I strive not: be that will perform'd!"

1:

May fays of Serapis,
Erudit at placide humanam per somnia mentem,
Nocturnaque quiete docet; nulloque labore
Hic tantum parta est pretiosa scientia, nullo
Excutitur studio verum. Mortalia corda
Tunc Deus iste docet, cum sunt minus apta doceri,
Cum nullum obsequium praestant, meritisque fatentur
Nil sese debere suis; tunc recta scientes
Cum nil scire valent. Non illo tempore sensus
Humanos forsan dignatur numen inire,
Cum propriis possunt per se discursibus uti,
Ne forte humana ratio divina coiret.
                    'Sup Lucani'.]

2: I have met with a singular tale to illustrate this spiritual theory of dreams.

Guntram, King of the Franks, was liberal to the poor, and he himself experienced the wonderful effects of divine liberality. For one day as he was hunting in a forest he was separated from his companions and arrived at a little stream of water with only one comrade of tried and approved fidelity. Here he found himself opprest by drowsiness, and reclining his head upon the servant's lap went to sleep. The servant witnessed a wonderful thing, for he saw a little beast ('bestiolam') creep out of the mouth of his sleeping master, and go immediately to the streamlet, which it vainly attempted to cross. The servant drew his sword and laid it across the water, over which the little beast easily past and crept into a hole of a mountain on the opposite side; from whence it made its appearance again in an hour, and returned by the same means into the King's mouth. The King then awakened, and told his companion that he had dreamt that he was arrived upon the bank of an immense river, which he had crossed by a bridge of iron, and from thence came to a mountain in which a great quantity of gold was concealed. When the King had concluded, the servant related what he had beheld, and they both went to examine the mountain, where upon digging they discovered an immense weight of gold.

I stumbled upon this tale in a book entitled SPHINX
'Theologico-Philosophica. Authore Johanne Heidfeldio, Ecclesiaste Ebersbachiano.' 1621.

The same story is in Matthew of Westminster; it is added that Guntram applied the treasures thus found to pious uses.

For the truth of this theory there is the evidence of a Monkish miracle. When Thurcillus was about to follow St. Julian and visit the world of souls, his guide said to him, "let thy body rest in the bed for thy spirit only is about to depart with me; and lest the body should appear dead, I will send into it a vital breath."

The body however by a strange sympathy was affected like the spirit; for when the foul and fetid smoke that arose from tithes witheld, had nearly suffocated Thurcillus, and made him cough twice, those who were near his body said that it coughed twice about the same time.

'Matthew Paris'.]

3: The Bastille. The expression is in one of Fuller's works, an Author from whose quaintness and ingenuity I have always found amusement, and sometimes assistance.

4: These lines strongly resemble a passage in the Pharonnida of William Chamberlayne, a Poet who has told an interesting story in uncouth rhymes, and mingled sublimity of thought and beauty of expression, with the quaintest conceits, and most awkward inversions.

> On a rock more high
> Than Nature's common surface, she beholds
> The Mansion house of Fate, which thus unfolds

Its sacred mysteries. A trine within
A quadrate placed, both these encompast in
A perfect circle was its form; but what
Its matter was, for us to wonder at,
Is undiscovered left. A Tower there stands
At every angle, where Time's fatal hands
The impartial PARCAE dwell; i' the first she sees
CLOTHO the kindest of the Destinies,
From immaterial essences to cull
The seeds of life, and of them frame the wool
For LACHESIS to spin; about her flie
Myriads of souls, that yet want flesh to lie
Warm'd with their functions in, whose strength bestows
That power by which man ripe for misery grows.

Her next of objects was that glorious tower
Where that swift-fingered Nymph that spares no hour
From mortals' service, draws the various threads
Of life in several lengths; to weary beds
Of age extending some, whilst others in
Their infancy are broke: 'some blackt in sin,
Others, the favorites of Heaven, from whence
Their origin, candid with innocence;
Some purpled in afflictions, others dyed
In sanguine pleasures': some in glittering pride
Spun to adorn the earth, whilst others wear
Rags of deformity, but knots of care
No thread was wholly free from. Next to this
Fair glorious tower, was placed that black abyss
Of dreadful ATROPOS, the baleful seat
Of death and horrour, in each room repleat
With lazy damps, loud groans, and the sad sight
Of pale grim Ghosts, those terrours of the night.
To this, the last stage that the winding clew
Of Life can lead mortality unto,
FEAR was the dreadful Porter, which let in
All guests sent thither by destructive sin.

It is possible that I may have written from the recollection of this passage. The conceit is the same, and I willingly attribute it to Chamberlayne, a Poet to whom I am indebted for many hours of delight, and whom I one day hope to rescue from undeserved oblivion.

THE SECOND BOOK

She spake, and lo! celestial radiance beam'd
Amid the air, such odors wafting now
As erst came blended with the evening gale,
From Eden's bowers of bliss. An angel form
Stood by the Maid; his wings, etherial white,
Flash'd like the diamond in the noon-tide sun,
Dazzling her mortal eye: all else appear'd
Her THEODORE.
   Amazed she saw: the Fiend
Was fled, and on her ear the well-known voice
Sounded, tho' now more musically sweet
Than ever yet had thrill'd her charmed soul,
When eloquent Affection fondly told
The day-dreams of delight.
    "Beloved Maid!
Lo! I am with thee! still thy Theodore!
Hearts in the holy bands of Love combin'd,
Death has no power to sever. Thou art mine!
A little while and thou shalt dwell with me
In scenes where Sorrow is not. Cheerily
Tread thou the path that leads thee to the grave,
Rough tho' it be and painful, for the grave
Is but the threshold of Eternity.

Favour'd of Heaven! to thee is given to view
These secret realms. The bottom of the abyss
Thou treadest, Maiden! Here the dungeons are
Where bad men learn repentance; souls diseased
Must have their remedy; and where disease
Is rooted deep, the remedy is long
Perforce, and painful."
    Thus the Spirit spake,
And led the Maid along a narrow path,
Dark gleaming to the light of far-off flames,
More dread than darkness. Soon the distant sound
Of clanking anvils, and the lengthened breath
Provoking fire are heard: and now they reach
A wide expanded den where all around
Tremendous furnaces, with hellish blaze,
Flamed dreadful. At the heaving bellows stood
The meagre form of Care, and as he blew
To augment the fire, the fire augmented scorch'd
His wretched limbs: sleepless for ever thus

He toil'd and toil'd, of toil to reap no end
But endless toil and never-ending woe.

An aged man went round the infernal vault,
Urging his workmen to their ceaseless task:
White were his locks, as is the wintry snow
On hoar Plinlimmon's head. A golden staff
His steps supported; powerful talisman,
Which whoso feels shall never feel again
The tear of Pity, or the throb of Love.
Touch'd but by this, the massy gates give way,
The buttress trembles, and the guarded wall,
Guarded in vain, submits. Him heathens erst
Had deified, and bowed the suppliant knee
To Plutus. Nor are now his votaries few,
Tho' he the Blessed Teacher of mankind
Hath said, that easier thro' the needle's eye
Shall the huge camel [1] pass, than the rich man
Enter the gates of heaven. "Ye cannot serve
Your God, and worship Mammon."
                "Missioned Maid!"
So spake the Angel, "know that these, whose hands
Round each white furnace ply the unceasing toil,
Were Mammon's slaves on earth. They did not spare
To wring from Poverty the hard-earn'd mite,
They robb'd the orphan's pittance, they could see
Want's asking eye unmoved; and therefore these,
Ranged round the furnace, still must persevere
In Mammon's service; scorched by these fierce fires,
And frequent deluged by the o'erboiling ore:
Yet still so framed, that oft to quench their thirst
Unquenchable, large draughts of molten [2] gold
They drink insatiate, still with pain renewed,
Pain to destroy."
            So saying, her he led
Forth from the dreadful cavern to a cell,
Brilliant with gem-born light. The rugged walls
Part gleam'd with gold, and part with silver ore
A milder radiance shone. The Carbuncle
There its strong lustre like the flamy sun
Shot forth irradiate; from the earth beneath,
And from the roof a diamond light emits;
Rubies and amethysts their glows commix'd
With the gay topaz, and the softer ray
Shot from the sapphire, and the emerald's hue,

And bright pyropus.
           There on golden seats,
A numerous, sullen, melancholy train
Sat silent. "Maiden, these," said Theodore,
Are they who let the love of wealth absorb
All other passions; in their souls that vice
Struck deeply-rooted, like the poison-tree
That with its shade spreads barrenness around.
These, Maid! were men by no atrocious crime
Blacken'd, no fraud, nor ruffian violence:
Men of fair dealing, and respectable
On earth, but such as only for themselves
Heap'd up their treasures, deeming all their wealth
Their own, and given to them, by partial Heaven,
To bless them only: therefore here they sit,
Possessed of gold enough, and by no pain
Tormented, save the knowledge of the bliss
They lost, and vain repentance. Here they dwell,
Loathing these useless treasures, till the hour
Of general restitution."
           Thence they past,
And now arrived at such a gorgeous dome,
As even the pomp of Eastern opulence
Could never equal: wandered thro' its halls
A numerous train; some with the red-swoln eye
Of riot, and intemperance-bloated cheek;
Some pale and nerveless, and with feeble step,
And eyes lack-lustre.
           Maiden? said her guide,
These are the wretched slaves of Appetite,
Curst with their wish enjoyed. The epicure
Here pampers his foul frame, till the pall'd sense
Loaths at the banquet; the voluptuous here
Plunge in the tempting torrent of delight,
And sink in misery. All they wish'd on earth,
Possessing here, whom have they to accuse,
But their own folly, for the lot they chose?
Yet, for that these injured themselves alone,
They to the house of PENITENCE may hie,
And, by a long and painful regimen,
To wearied Nature her exhausted powers
Restore, till they shall learn to form the wish
Of wisdom, and ALMIGHTY GOODNESS grants
That prize to him who seeks it."
           Whilst he spake,

The board is spread. With bloated paunch, and eye
Fat swoln, and legs whose monstrous size disgraced
The human form divine, their caterer,
Hight GLUTTONY, set forth the smoking feast.
And by his side came on a brother form,
With fiery cheek of purple hue, and red
And scurfy-white, mix'd motley; his gross bulk,
Like some huge hogshead shapen'd, as applied.
Him had antiquity with mystic rites
Ador'd, to him the sons of Greece, and thine
Imperial Rome, on many an altar pour'd
The victim blood, with godlike titles graced,
BACCHUS, or DIONUSUS; son of JOVE,
Deem'd falsely, for from FOLLY'S ideot form
He sprung, what time MADNESS, with furious hand,
Seiz'd on the laughing female. At one birth
She brought the brethren, menial here, above
Reigning with sway supreme, and oft they hold
High revels: mid the Monastery's gloom,
The sacrifice is spread, when the grave voice
Episcopal, proclaims approaching day
Of visitation, or Churchwardens meet
To save the wretched many from the gripe
Of eager Poverty, or mid thy halls
Of London, mighty Mayor! rich Aldermen,
Of coming feast hold converse.
     Otherwhere,
For tho' allied in nature as in blood,
They hold divided sway, his brother lifts
His spungy sceptre. In the noble domes
Of Princes, and state-wearied Ministers,
Maddening he reigns; and when the affrighted mind
Casts o'er a long career of guilt and blood
Its eye reluctant, then his aid is sought
To lull the worm of Conscience to repose.
He too the halls of country Squires frequents,
But chiefly loves the learned gloom that shades
Thy offspring Rhedycina! and thy walls,
Granta! nightly libations there to him
Profuse are pour'd, till from the dizzy brain
Triangles, Circles, Parallelograms,
Moods, Tenses, Dialects, and Demigods,
And Logic and Theology are swept
By the red deluge.
     Unmolested there

He reigns; till comes at length the general feast,
Septennial sacrifice; then when the sons
Of England meet, with watchful care to chuse
Their delegates, wise, independent men,
Unbribing and unbrib'd, and cull'd to guard
Their rights and charters from the encroaching grasp
Of greedy Power: then all the joyful land
Join in his sacrifices, so inspir'd
To make the important choice.
                    The observing Maid
Address'd her guide, "These Theodore, thou sayest
Are men, who pampering their foul appetites,
Injured themselves alone. But where are they,
The worst of villains, viper-like, who coil
Around the guileless female, so to sting
The heart that loves them?"
                    "Them," the spirit replied,
A long and dreadful punishment awaits.
For when the prey of want and infamy,
Lower and lower still the victim sinks,
Even to the depth of shame, not one lewd word,
One impious imprecation from her lips
Escapes, nay not a thought of evil lurks
In the polluted mind, that does not plead
Before the throne of Justice, thunder-tongued
Against the foul Seducer."
                    Now they reach'd
The house of PENITENCE. CREDULITY
Stood at the gate, stretching her eager head
As tho' to listen; on her vacant face,
A smile that promis'd premature assent;
Tho' her REGRET behind, a meagre Fiend,
Disciplin'd sorely.
                    Here they entered in,
And now arrived where, as in study tranced,
She sat, the Mistress of the Dome. Her face
Spake that composed severity, that knows
No angry impulse, no weak tenderness,
Resolved and calm. Before her lay that Book
That hath the words of Life; and as she read,
Sometimes a tear would trickle down her cheek,
Tho' heavenly joy beam'd in her eye the while.

Leaving her undisturb'd, to the first ward
Of this great Lazar-house, the Angel led

The favour'd Maid of Orleans. Kneeling down
On the hard stone that their bare knees had worn,
In sackcloth robed, a numerous train appear'd:
Hard-featured some, and some demurely grave;
Yet such expression stealing from the eye,
As tho', that only naked, all the rest
Was one close fitting mask. A scoffing Fiend,
For Fiend he was, tho' wisely serving here
Mock'd at his patients, and did often pour
Ashes upon them, and then bid them say
Their prayers aloud, and then he louder laughed:
For these were Hypocrites, on earth revered
As holy ones, who did in public tell
Their beads, and make long prayers, and cross themselves,
And call themselves most miserable sinners,
That so they might be deem'd most pious saints;
And go all filth, and never let a smile
Bend their stern muscles, gloomy, sullen men,
Barren of all affection, and all this
To please their God, forsooth! and therefore SCORN
Grinn'd at his patients, making them repeat
Their solemn farce, with keenest raillery
Tormenting; but if earnest in their prayer,
They pour'd the silent sorrows of the soul
To Heaven, then did they not regard his mocks
Which then came painless, and HUMILITY
Soon rescued them, and led to PENITENCE,
That She might lead to Heaven.

    From thence they came,
Where, in the next ward, a most wretched band
Groan'd underneath the bitter tyranny
Of a fierce Daemon. His coarse hair was red,
Pale grey his eyes, and blood-shot; and his face
Wrinkled by such a smile as Malice wears
In ecstacy. Well-pleased he went around,
Plunging his dagger in the hearts of some,
Or probing with a poison'd lance their breasts,
Or placing coals of fire within their wounds;
Or seizing some within his mighty grasp,
He fix'd them on a stake, and then drew back,
And laugh'd to see them writhe.
     "These," said the Spirit,
Are taught by CRUELTY, to loath the lives
They led themselves. Here are those wicked men

Who loved to exercise their tyrant power
On speechless brutes; bad husbands undergo
A long purgation here; the traffickers
In human flesh here too are disciplined.
Till by their suffering they have equall'd all
The miseries they inflicted, all the mass
Of wretchedness caused by the wars they waged,
The towns they burnt, for they who bribe to war
Are guilty of the blood, the widows left
In want, the slave or led to suicide,
Or murdered by the foul infected air
Of his close dungeon, or more sad than all,
His virtue lost, his very soul enslaved,
And driven by woe to wickedness.
     These next,
Whom thou beholdest in this dreary room,
So sullen, and with such an eye of hate
Each on the other scowling, these have been
False friends. Tormented by their own dark thoughts
Here they dwell: in the hollow of their hearts
There is a worm that feeds, and tho' thou seest
That skilful leech who willingly would heal
The ill they suffer, judging of all else
By their own evil standard, they suspect
The aid be vainly proffers, lengthening thus
By vice its punishment."
    "But who are these,"
The Maid exclaim'd, "that robed in flowing lawn,
And mitred, or in scarlet, and in caps
Like Cardinals, I see in every ward,
Performing menial service at the beck
Of all who bid them?"
    Theodore replied,
These men are they who in the name of CHRIST
Did heap up wealth, and arrogating power,
Did make men bow the knee, and call themselves
Most Reverend Graces and Right Reverend Lords.
They dwelt in palaces, in purple clothed,
And in fine linen: therefore are they here;
And tho' they would not minister on earth,
Here penanced they perforce must minister:
For he, the lowly man of Nazareth,
Hath said, his kingdom is not of the world."
So Saying on they past, and now arrived
Where such a hideous ghastly groupe abode,

That the Maid gazed with half-averting eye,
And shudder'd: each one was a loathly corpse,
The worm did banquet on his putrid prey,
Yet had they life and feeling exquisite
Tho' motionless and mute.
    "Most wretched men
Are these, the angel cried. These, JOAN, are bards,
Whose loose lascivious lays perpetuate
Who sat them down, deliberately lewd,
So to awake and pamper lust in minds
Unborn; and therefore foul of body now
As then they were of soul, they here abide
Long as the evil works they left on earth
Shall live to taint mankind. A dreadful doom!
Yet amply merited by that bad man
Who prostitutes the sacred gift of song!"
And now they reached a huge and massy pile,
Massy it seem'd, and yet in every blast
As to its ruin shook. There, porter fit,
REMORSE for ever his sad vigils kept.
Pale, hollow-eyed, emaciate, sleepless wretch.
Inly he groan'd, or, starting, wildly shriek'd,
Aye as the fabric tottering from its base,
Threatened its fall, and so expectant still
Lived in the dread of danger still delayed.

They enter'd there a large and lofty dome,
O'er whose black marble sides a dim drear light
Struggled with darkness from the unfrequent lamp.
Enthroned around, the MURDERERS OF MANKIND,
Monarchs, the great! the glorious! the august!
Each bearing on his brow a crown of fire,
Sat stern and silent. Nimrod he was there,
First King the mighty hunter; and that Chief
Who did belie his mother's fame, that so
He might be called young Ammon. In this court
Caesar was crown'd, accurst liberticide;
And he who murdered Tully, that cold villain,
Octavius, tho' the courtly minion's lyre
Hath hymn'd his praise, tho' Maro sung to him,
And when Death levelled to original clay
The royal carcase, FLATTERY, fawning low,
Fell at his feet, and worshipped the new God.
Titus [3] was here, the Conqueror of the Jews,
He the Delight of human-kind misnamed;

Caesars and Soldans, Emperors and Kings,
Here they were all, all who for glory fought,
Here in the COURT OF GLORY, reaping now
The meed they merited.
            As gazing round
The Virgin mark'd the miserable train,
A deep and hollow voice from one went forth;
"Thou who art come to view our punishment,
Maiden of Orleans! hither turn thine eyes,
For I am he whose bloody victories
Thy power hath rendered vain. Lo! I am here,
The hero conqueror of Azincour,
HENRY OF ENGLAND!--wretched that I am,
I might have reigned in happiness and peace,
My coffers full, my subjects undisturb'd,
And PLENTY and PROSPERITY had loved
To dwell amongst them: but mine eye beheld
The realm of France, by faction tempest-torn,
And therefore I did think that it would fall
An easy prey. I persecuted those
Who taught new doctrines, tho' they taught the truth:
And when I heard of thousands by the sword
Cut off, or blasted by the pestilence,
I calmly counted up my proper gains,
And sent new herds to slaughter. Temperate
Myself, no blood that mutinied, no vice
Tainting my private life, I sent abroad
MURDER and RAPE; and therefore am I doom'd,
Like these imperial Sufferers, crown'd with fire,
Here to remain, till Man's awaken'd eye
Shall see the genuine blackness of our deeds,
And warn'd by them, till the whole human race,
Equalling in bliss the aggregate we caus'd
Of wretchedness, shall form One Brotherhood, One Universal Family
Of Love."

1: In the former edition I had substituted 'cable' instead of 'camel'. The alteration would not be worth noticing were it not for the circumstance which occasioned it. 'Facilius elephas per foramen acus', is among the Hebrew adages collected by Drusius; the same metaphor is found in two other Jewish proverbs, and this appears to determine the signification of [Greek (transliterated): chamaelos]. Matt. 19. 24.]

2: The same idea, and almost the same words are in an old play by John Ford. The passage is a very fine one:

> Ay, you are wretched, miserably wretched,
> Almost condemn'd alive! There is a place,
> (List daughter!) in a black and hollow vault,
> Where day is never seen; there shines no sun,
> But flaming horror of consuming fires;
> A lightless sulphur, choak'd with smoaky foggs
> Of an infected darkness. In this place
> Dwell many thousand thousand sundry sorts
> Of never-dying deaths; there damned souls
> Roar without pity, there are gluttons fed
> With toads and adders; there is burning oil
> Pour'd down the drunkard's throat, 'the usurer
> Is forced to sup whole draughts of molten gold';
> There is the murderer for ever stabb'd,
> Yet can he never die; there lies the wanton
> On racks of burning steel, whilst in his soul
> He feels the torment of his raging lust.
>
> '"Tis Pity she's a Whore.'

I wrote this passage when very young, and the idea, trite as it is, was new to me. It occurs I believe in most descriptions of hell, and perhaps owes its origin to the fate of Crassus.

After this picture of horrors, the reader may perhaps be pleased with one more pleasantly fanciful:

> O call me home again dear Chief! and put me
> To yoking foxes, milking of he-goats,
> Pounding of water in a mortar, laving
> The sea dry with a nutshell, gathering all
> The leaves are fallen this autumn--making ropes of sand,
> Catching the winds together in a net,
> Mustering of ants, and numbering atoms, all
> That Hell and you thought exquisite torments, rather
> Than stay me here a thought more. I would sooner
> Keep fleas within a circle, and be accomptant
> A thousand year which of 'em, and how far
> Outleap'd the other, than endure a minute
> Such as I have within.
>
> B. JONSON. 'The Devil is an Ass.'

3: During the siege of Jerusalem, "the Roman commander, 'with a generous clemency, that inseparable attendant on true heroism, 'laboured incessantly, and to the very last moment, to preserve the place. With this view, he again

and again intreated the tyrants to surrender and save their lives. With the same view also, after carrying the second wall the siege was intermitted four days: to rouse their fears, 'prisoners, to the number of five hundred, or more were crucified daily before the walls; till space', Josephus says, 'was wanting for the crosses, and crosses for the captives'."
From the Hampton Lectures of RALPH CHURTON.

    If any of my readers should enquire why Titus Vespasian, the Delight of Mankind, is placed in such a situation,--I answer, for "His Generousclemency, That Inseparable Attendant On True Heroism!

THE THIRD BOOK

The Maiden, musing on the Warrior's words,
Turn'd from the Hall of Glory. Now they reach'd
A cavern, at whose mouth a Genius stood,
In front a beardless youth, whose smiling eye
Beam'd promise, but behind, withered and old,
And all unlovely. Underneath his feet
Lay records trampled, and the laurel wreath
Now rent and faded: in his hand he held
An hour-glass, and as fall the restless sands,
So pass the lives of men. By him they past
Along the darksome cave, and reach'd a stream,
Still rolling onward its perpetual waves,
Noiseless and undisturbed. Here they ascend
A Bark unpiloted, that down the flood,
Borne by the current, rush'd. The circling stream,
Returning to itself, an island form'd;
Nor had the Maiden's footsteps ever reach'd
The insulated coast, eternally
Rapt round the endless course; but Theodore
Drove with an angel's will the obedient bark.

They land, a mighty fabric meets their eyes,
Seen by its gem-born light. Of adamant
The pile was framed, for ever to abide
Firm in eternal strength. Before the gate
Stood eager EXPECTATION, as to list
The half-heard murmurs issuing from within,
Her mouth half-open'd, and her head stretch'd forth.
On the other side there stood an aged Crone,
Listening to every breath of air; she knew
Vague suppositions and uncertain dreams,
Of what was soon to come, for she would mark
The paley glow-worm's self-created light,
And argue thence of kingdoms overthrown,
And desolated nations; ever fill'd
With undetermin'd terror, as she heard
Or distant screech-owl, or the regular beat
Of evening death-watch.   "Maid," the Spirit cried,
Here, robed in shadows, dwells FUTURITY.
There is no eye hath seen her secret form,
For round the MOTHER OF TIME, unpierced mists
Aye hover. Would'st thou read the book of Fate,

Enter."
  The Damsel for a moment paus'd,
Then to the Angel spake: "All-gracious Heaven!
Benignant in withholding, hath denied
To man that knowledge. I, in faith assured,
That he, my heavenly Father, for the best
Ordaineth all things, in that faith remain
Contented."
  "Well and wisely hast thou said,
So Theodore replied; "and now O Maid!
Is there amid this boundless universe
One whom thy soul would visit? is there place
To memory dear, or visioned out by hope,
Where thou would'st now be present? form the wish,
And I am with thee, there."
  His closing speech
Yet sounded on her ear, and lo! they stood
Swift as the sudden thought that guided them,
Within the little cottage that she loved.
"He sleeps! the good man sleeps!" enrapt she cried,
As bending o'er her Uncle's lowly bed
Her eye retraced his features. "See the beads
That never morn nor night he fails to tell,
Remembering me, his child, in every prayer.
Oh! quiet be thy sleep, thou dear old man!
Good Angels guard thy rest! and when thine hour
Is come, as gently mayest thou wake to life,
As when thro' yonder lattice the next sun
Shall bid thee to thy morning orisons!
Thy voice is heard, the Angel guide rejoin'd,
He sees thee in his dreams, he hears thee breathe
Blessings, and pleasant is the good man's rest.
Thy fame has reached him, for who has not heard
Thy wonderous exploits? and his aged heart
Hath felt the deepest joy that ever yet
Made his glad blood flow fast. Sleep on old Claude!
Peaceful, pure Spirit, be thy sojourn here,
And short and soon thy passage to that world
Where friends shall part no more!
  "Does thy soul own
No other wish? or sleeps poor Madelon
Forgotten in her grave? seest thou yon star,"
The Spirit pursued, regardless of her eye
That look'd reproach; "seest thou that evening star
Whose lovely light so often we beheld

From yonder woodbine porch? how have we gazed
Into the dark deep sky, till the baffled soul,
Lost in the infinite, returned, and felt
The burthen of her bodily load, and yearned
For freedom! Maid, in yonder evening slar
Lives thy departed friend. I read that glance,
And we are there!"
          He said and they had past
The immeasurable space.
              Then on her ear
The lonely song of adoration rose,
Sweet as the cloister'd virgins vesper hymn,
Whose spirit, happily dead to earthly hopes
Already lives in Heaven. Abrupt the song
Ceas'd, tremulous and quick a cry
Of joyful wonder rous'd the astonish'd Maid,
And instant Madelon was in her arms;
No airy form, no unsubstantial shape,
She felt her friend, she prest her to her heart,
Their tears of rapture mingled.
              She drew back
And eagerly she gazed on Madelon,
Then fell upon her neck again and wept.
No more she saw the long-drawn lines of grief,
The emaciate form, the hue of sickliness,
The languid eye: youth's loveliest freshness now
Mantled her cheek, whose every lineament
Bespake the soul at rest, a holy calm,
A deep and full tranquillity of bliss.

"Thou then art come, my first and dearest friend!"
The well known voice of Madelon began,
"Thou then art come! and was thy pilgrimage
So short on earth? and was it painful too,
Painful and short as mine? but blessed they
Who from the crimes and miseries of the world
Early escape!"
          "Nay," Theodore replied,
She hath not yet fulfill'd her mortal work.
Permitted visitant from earth she comes
To see the seat of rest, and oftentimes
In sorrow shall her soul remember this,
And patient of the transitory woe
Partake the anticipated peace again."
"Soon be that work perform'd!" the Maid exclaimed,

"O Madelon! O Theodore! my soul,
Spurning the cold communion of the world,
Will dwell with you! but I shall patiently,
Yea even with joy, endure the allotted ills
Of which the memory in this better state
Shall heighten bliss. That hour of agony,
When, Madelon, I felt thy dying grasp,
And from thy forehead wiped the dews of death,
The very horrors of that hour assume
A shape that now delights."
                      "O earliest friend!
I too remember," Madelon replied,
"That hour, thy looks of watchful agony,
The suppressed grief that struggled in thine eye
Endearing love's last kindness. Thou didst know
With what a deep and melancholy joy
I felt the hour draw on: but who can speak
The unutterable transport, when mine eyes,
As from a long and dreary dream, unclosed
Amid this peaceful vale, unclos'd on him,
My Arnaud! he had built me up a bower,
A bower of rest.--See, Maiden, where he comes,
His manly lineaments, his beaming eye
The same, but now a holier innocence
Sits on his cheek, and loftier thoughts illume
The enlighten'd glance."
                    They met, what joy was theirs
He best can feel, who for a dear friend dead
Has wet the midnight pillow with his tears.

Fair was the scene around; an ample vale
Whose mountain circle at the distant verge
Lay softened on the sight; the near ascent
Rose bolder up, in part abrupt and bare,
Part with the ancient majesty of woods
Adorn'd, or lifting high its rocks sublime.
The river's liquid radiance roll'd beneath,
Beside the bower of Madelon it wound
A broken stream, whose shallows, tho' the waves
Roll'd on their way with rapid melody,
A child might tread. Behind, an orange grove
Its gay green foliage starr'd with golden fruit;
But with what odours did their blossoms load
The passing gale of eve! less thrilling sweet
Rose from the marble's perforated floor,

Where kneeling at her prayers, the Moorish queen
Inhaled the cool delight, [1] and whilst she asked
The Prophet for his promised paradise,
Shaped from the present scene its utmost joys.
A goodly scene! fair as that faery land
Where Arthur lives, by ministering spirits borne
From Camlan's bloody banks; or as the groves
Of earliest Eden, where, so legends say,
Enoch abides, and he who rapt away
By fiery steeds, and chariotted in fire,
Past in his mortal form the eternal ways;
And John, beloved of Christ, enjoying there
The beatific vision, sometimes seen
The distant dawning of eternal day,
Till all things be fulfilled.
                "Survey this scene!"
So Theodore address'd the Maid of Arc,
"There is no evil here, no wretchedness,
It is the Heaven of those who nurst on earth
Their nature's gentlest feelings. Yet not here
Centering their joys, but with a patient hope,
Waiting the allotted hour when capable
Of loftier callings, to a better state
They pass; and hither from that better state
Frequent they come, preserving so those ties
That thro' the infinite progressiveness
Complete our perfect bliss.
                "Even such, so blest,
Save that the memory of no sorrows past
Heightened the present joy, our world was once,
In the first aera of its innocence
Ere man had learnt to bow the knee to man.
Was there a youth whom warm affection fill'd,
He spake his honest heart; the earliest fruits
His toil produced, the sweetest flowers that deck'd
The sunny bank, he gather'd for the maid,
Nor she disdain'd the gift; for VICE not yet
Had burst the dungeons of her hell, and rear'd
Those artificial boundaries that divide
Man from his species. State of blessedness!
Till that ill-omen'd hour when Cain's stern son
Delved in the bowels of the earth for gold,
Accursed bane of virtue! of such force
As poets feign dwelt in the Gorgon's locks,
Which whoso saw, felt instant the life-blood

Cold curdle in his veins, the creeping flesh
Grew stiff with horror, and the heart forgot
To beat. Accursed hour! for man no more
To JUSTICE paid his homage, but forsook
Her altars, and bow'd down before the shrine
Of WEALTH and POWER, the Idols he had made.
Then HELL enlarged herself, her gates flew wide,
Her legion fiends rush'd forth. OPPRESSION came
Whose frown is desolation, and whose breath
Blasts like the Pestilence; and POVERTY,
A meagre monster, who with withering touch
Makes barren all the better part of man,
MOTHER OF MISERIES. Then the goodly earth
Which God had fram'd for happiness, became
One theatre of woe, and all that God
Had given to bless free men, these tyrant fiends
His bitterest curses made. Yet for the best
Hath he ordained all things, the ALL-WISE!
For by experience rous'd shall man at length
Dash down his Moloch-Idols, Samson-like
And burst his fetters, only strong whilst strong
Believed. Then in the bottomless abyss
OPPRESSION shall be chain'd, and POVERTY
Die, and with her, her brood of Miseries;
And VIRTUE and EQUALITY preserve
The reign of LOVE, and Earth shall once again
Be Paradise, whilst WISDOM shall secure
The state of bliss which IGNORANCE betrayed."

"Oh age of happiness!" the Maid exclaim'd,
Roll fast thy current, Time till that blest age
Arrive! and happy thou my Theodore,
Permitted thus to see the sacred depths
Of wisdom!"
              "Such," the blessed Spirit replied,
Beloved! such our lot; allowed to range
The vast infinity, progressive still
In knowledge and encreasing blessedness,
This our united portion. Thou hast yet
A little while to sojourn amongst men:
I will be with thee! there shall not a breeze
Wanton around thy temples, on whose wing
I will not hover near! and at that hour
When from its fleshly sepulchre let loose,
Thy phoenix soul shall soar, O best-beloved!

I will be with thee in thine agonies,
And welcome thee to life and happiness,
Eternal infinite beatitude!"

He spake, and led her near a straw-roof'd cot,
LOVE'S Palace. By the Virtues circled there,
The cherub listen'd to such melodies,
As aye, when one good deed is register'd
Above, re-echo in the halls of Heaven.
LABOUR was there, his crisp locks floating loose,
Clear was his cheek, and beaming his full eye,
And strong his arm robust; the wood-nymph HEALTH
Still follow'd on his path, and where he trod
Fresh flowers and fruits arose. And there was HOPE,
The general friend; and PITY, whose mild eye
Wept o'er the widowed dove; and, loveliest form,
Majestic CHASTITY, whose sober smile
Delights and awes the soul; a laurel wreath
Restrain'd her tresses, and upon her breast
The snow-drop [2] hung its head, that seem'd to grow
Spontaneous, cold and fair: still by the maid
LOVE went submiss, wilh eye more dangerous
Than fancied basilisk to wound whoe'er
Too bold approached; yet anxious would he read
Her every rising wish, then only pleased
When pleasing. Hymning him the song was rais'd.

"Glory to thee whose vivifying power
Pervades all Nature's universal frame!
Glory to thee CREATOR LOVE! to thee,
Parent of all the smiling CHARITIES,
That strew the thorny path of Life with flowers!
Glory to thee PRESERVER! to thy praise
The awakened woodlands echo all the day
Their living melody; and warbling forth
To thee her twilight song, the Nightingale
Holds the lone Traveller from his way, or charms
The listening Poet's ear. Where LOVE shall deign
To fix his seat, there blameless PLEASURE sheds
Her roseate dews; CONTENT will sojourn there,
And HAPPINESS behold AFFECTION'S eye
Gleam with the Mother's smile. Thrice happy he
Who feels thy holy power! he shall not drag,
Forlorn and friendless, along Life's long path
To Age's drear abode; he shall not waste

The bitter evening of his days unsooth'd;
But HOPE shall cheer his hours of Solitude,
And VICE shall vainly strive to wound his breast,
That bears that talisman; and when he meets
The eloquent eye of TENDERNESS, and hears
The bosom-thrilling music of her voice;
The joy he feels shall purify his Soul,
And imp it for anticipated Heaven."

1: In the cabinet of the Alhambra where the Queen used to dress and say her prayers, and which is still an enchanting sight, there is a slab of marble full of small holes, through which perfumes exhaled that were kept constantly burning beneath. The doors and windows are disposed so as to afford the most agreeable prospects, and to throw a soft yet lively light upon the eyes. Fresh currents of air too are admitted, so as to renew every instant the delicious coolness of this apartment.
    (From the sketch of the History of the Spanish Moors, prefixed toFlorian's Gonsalvo of Cordova).
2: "The grave matron does not perceive how time has impaired her charms, but decks her faded bosom with the same snow-drop that seems to grow on the breast of the Virgin." P.H.]

THE ROSE

Betwene the Cytee and the Chirche of Bethlehem, is the felde Floridus, that is to seyne, the feld florisched. For als moche as a fayre Mayden was blamed with wrong and sclaundred, that sche hadde don fornicacioun, for whiche cause sche was demed to the dethe, and to be brent in that place, to the whiche sche was ladd. And as the fyre began to brenne about hire, she made hire preyeres to oure Lord, that als wissely as sche was not gylty of that synne, that he wold help hire, and make it to be knowen to alle men of his mercyfulle grace; and whanne she had thus seyd, sche entered into the fuyer, and anon was the fuyer quenched and oute, and the brondes that weren brennynge, becomen white Roseres, fulle of roses, and theise weren the first Roseres and roses, bothe white and rede, that evere ony man saughe.

And thus was this Maiden saved be the Grace of God.

'The Voiage and Travaile of Sir John Maundevile'.

THE ROSE

Nay EDITH! spare the rose!--it lives--it lives,
It feels the noon-tide sun, and drinks refresh'd
The dews of night; let not thy gentle hand
Tear sunder its life-fibres and destroy
The sense of being!--why that infidel smile?
Come, I will bribe thee to be merciful,
And thou shall have a tale of other times,
For I am skill'd in legendary lore,
So thou wilt let it live. There was a time
Ere this, the freshest sweetest flower that blooms,
Bedeck'd the bowers of earth. Thou hast not heard
How first by miracle its fragrant leaves
Spread to the sun their blushing loveliness.

There dwelt at Bethlehem a Jewish maid
And Zillah was her name, so passing fair
That all Judea spake the damsel's praise.
He who had seen her eyes' dark radiance
How quick it spake the soul, and what a soul
Beam'd in its mild effulgence, woe was he!
For not in solitude, for not in crowds,
Might he escape remembrance, or avoid
Her imaged form that followed every where,
And fill'd the heart, and fix'd the absent eye.
Woe was he, for her bosom own'd no love
Save the strong ardours of religious zeal,
For Zillah on her God had centered all
Her spirit's deep affections. So for her
Her tribes-men sigh'd in vain, yet reverenced
The obdurate virtue that destroyed their hopes.

One man there was, a vain and wretched man,
Who saw, desired, despair'd, and hated her.
His sensual eye had gloated on her cheek
Even till the flush of angry modesty
Gave it new charms, and made him gloat the more.
She loath'd the man, for Hamuel's eye was bold,
And the strong workings of brute selfishness
Had moulded his broad features; and she fear'd
The bitterness of wounded vanity
That with a fiendish hue would overcast
His faint and lying smile. Nor vain her fear,
For Hamuel vowed revenge and laid a plot

Against her virgin fame. He spread abroad
Whispers that travel fast, and ill reports
That soon obtain belief; that Zillah's eye
When in the temple heaven-ward it was rais'd
Did swim with rapturous zeal, but there were those
Who had beheld the enthusiast's melting glance
With other feelings fill'd; that 'twas a task
Of easy sort to play the saint by day
Before the public eye, but that all eyes
Were closed at night; that Zillah's life was foul,
Yea forfeit to the law.
    Shame--shame to man
That he should trust so easily the tongue
That stabs another's fame! the ill report
Was heard, repeated, and believed,--and soon,
For Hamuel by most damned artifice
Produced such semblances of guilt, the Maid
Was judged to shameful death.
    Without the walls
There was a barren field; a place abhorr'd,
For it was there where wretched criminals
Were done to die; and there they built the stake,
And piled the fuel round, that should consume
The accused Maid, abandon'd, as it seem'd,
By God and man. The assembled Bethlemites
Beheld the scene, and when they saw the Maid
Bound to the stake, with what calm holiness
She lifted up her patient looks to Heaven,
They doubted of her guilt. With other thoughts
Stood Hamuel near the pile, him savage joy
Led thitherward, but now within his heart
Unwonted feelings stirr'd, and the first pangs
Of wakening guilt, anticipating Hell.
The eye of Zillah as it glanced around
Fell on the murderer once, but not in wrath;
And therefore like a dagger it had fallen,
Had struck into his soul a cureless wound.
Conscience! thou God within us! not in the hour
Of triumph, dost thou spare the guilty wretch,
Not in the hour of infamy and death
Forsake the virtuous! they draw near the stake--
And lo! the torch! hold hold your erring hands!
Yet quench the rising flames!--they rise! they spread!
They reach the suffering Maid! oh God protect

The innocent one!
            They rose, they spread, they raged--
The breath of God went forth; the ascending fire
Beneath its influence bent, and all its flames
In one long lightning flash collecting fierce,
Darted and blasted Hamuel--him alone.
Hark--what a fearful scream the multitude
Pour forth!--and yet more miracles! the stake
Buds out, and spreads its light green leaves and bowers
The innocent Maid, and roses bloom around,
Now first beheld since Paradise was lost,
And fill with Eden odours all the air.

THE COMPLAINTS OF THE POOR

And wherefore do the Poor complain?
  The rich man asked of me,--
Come walk abroad with me, I said
  And I will answer thee.

Twas evening and the frozen streets
  Were cheerless to behold,
And we were wrapt and coated well,
  And yet we were a-cold.

We met an old bare-headed man,
  His locks were few and white,
I ask'd him what he did abroad
  In that cold winter's night:

'Twas bitter keen indeed, he said,
  But at home no fire had he,
And therefore, he had come abroad
  To ask for charity.

We met a young bare-footed child,
  And she begg'd loud and bold,
I ask'd her what she did abroad
  When the wind it blew so cold;

She said her father was at home
  And he lay sick a-bed,
And therefore was it she was sent
  Abroad to beg for bread.

We saw a woman sitting down
  Upon a stone to rest,
She had a baby at her back
  And another at her breast;

I ask'd her why she loiter'd there
  When the wind it was so chill;
She turn'd her head and bade the child
  That scream'd behind be still.

She told us that her husband served
  A soldier, far away,
And therefore to her parish she

Was begging back her way.

We met a girl; her dress was loose
  And sunken was her eye,
Who with the wanton's hollow voice
  Address'd the passers by;

I ask'd her what there was in guilt
  That could her heart allure
To shame, disease, and late remorse?
  She answer'd, she was poor.

I turn'd me to the rich man then
  For silently stood he,
You ask'd me why the Poor complain,
  And these have answer'd thee.

METRICAL LETTER

WRITTEN from London.

    Margaret! my Cousin!--nay, you must not smile;
I love the homely and familiar phrase;
And I will call thee Cousin Margaret,
However quaint amid the measured line
The good old term appears. Oh! it looks ill
When delicate tongues disclaim old terms of kin,
Sirring and Madaming as civilly
As if the road between the heart and lips
Were such a weary and Laplandish way
That the poor travellers came to the red gates
Half frozen. Trust me Cousin Margaret,
For many a day my Memory has played
The creditor with me on your account,
And made me shame to think that I should owe
So long the debt of kindness. But in truth,
Like Christian on his pilgrimage, I bear
So heavy a pack of business, that albeit
I toil on mainly, in our twelve hours race
Time leaves me distanced. Loath indeed were I
That for a moment you should lay to me
Unkind neglect; mine, Margaret, is a heart
That smokes not, yet methinks there should be some
Who know how warm it beats. I am not one
Who can play off my smiles and courtesies
To every Lady of her lap dog tired
Who wants a play-thing; I am no sworn friend
Of half-an-hour, as apt to leave as love;
Mine are no mushroom feelings that spring up
At once without a seed and take no root,
Wiseliest distrusted. In a narrow sphere
The little circle of domestic life
I would be known and loved; the world beyond
Is not for me. But Margaret, sure I think
That you should know me well, for you and I
Grew up together, and when we look back
Upon old times our recollections paint
The same familiar faces. Did I wield
The wand of Merlin's magic I would make
Brave witchcraft. We would have a faery ship,
Aye, a new Ark, as in that other flood
That cleansed the sons of Anak from the earth,

The Sylphs should waft us to some goodly isle
Like that where whilome old Apollidon
Built up his blameless spell; and I would bid
The Sea Nymphs pile around their coral bowers,
That we might stand upon the beach, and mark
The far-off breakers shower their silver spray,
And hear the eternal roar whose pleasant sound
Told us that never mariner should reach
Our quiet coast. In such a blessed isle
We might renew the days of infancy,
And Life like a long childhood pass away,
Without one care. It may be, Margaret,
That I shall yet be gathered to my friends,
For I am not of those who live estranged
Of choice, till at the last they join their race
In the family vault. If so, if I should lose,
Like my old friend the Pilgrim, this huge pack
So heavy on my shoulders, I and mine
Will end our pilgrimage most pleasantly.
If not, if I should never get beyond
This Vanity town, there is another world
Where friends will meet. And often, Margaret,
I gaze at night into the boundless sky,
And think that I shall there be born again,
The exalted native of some better star;
And like the rude American I hope
To find in Heaven the things I loved on earth.

THE CROSS ROADS

The circumstance related in the following Ballad happened about forty years ago in a village adjacent to Bristol. A person who was present at the funeral, told me the story and the particulars of the interment, as I have versified them.

THE CROSS ROADS.

There was an old man breaking stones
  To mend the turnpike way,
He sat him down beside a brook
And out his bread and cheese he took,
  For now it was mid-day.

He lent his back against a post,
  His feet the brook ran by;
And there were water-cresses growing,
And pleasant was the water's flowing
  For he was hot and dry.

A soldier with his knapsack on
  Came travelling o'er the down,
The sun was strong and he was tired,
And of the old man he enquired
  How far to Bristol town.

Half an hour's walk for a young man
  By lanes and fields and stiles.
But you the foot-path do not know,
And if along the road you go
  Why then 'tis three good miles.

The soldier took his knapsack off
  For he was hot and dry;
And out his bread and cheese he took
And he sat down beside the brook
  To dine in company.

Old friend! in faith, the soldier says
  I envy you almost;
My shoulders have been sorely prest
And I should like to sit and rest,
  My back against that post.

In such a sweltering day as this
  A knapsack is the devil!
And if on t'other side I sat
It would not only spoil our chat
  But make me seem uncivil.

The old man laugh'd and moved. I wish
  It were a great-arm'd chair!
But this may help a man at need;
And yet it was a cursed deed
  That ever brought it there.

There's a poor girl lies buried here
  Beneath this very place.
The earth upon her corpse is prest
This stake is driven into her breast
  And a stone is on her face.

The soldier had but just lent back
  And now he half rose up.
There's sure no harm in dining here,
My friend? and yet to be sincere
  I should not like to sup.

God rest her! she is still enough
  Who sleeps beneath our feet!
The old man cried. No harm I trow
She ever did herself, tho' now
  She lies where four roads meet.

I have past by about that hour
  When men are not most brave,
It did not make my heart to fail,
And I have heard the nightingale
  Sing sweetly on her grave.

I have past by about that hour
  When Ghosts their freedom have,
But there was nothing here to fright,
And I have seen the glow-worm's light
  Shine on the poor girl's grave.

There's one who like a Christian lies
  Beneath the church-tree's shade;
I'd rather go a long mile round

Than pass at evening thro' the ground
　　　Wherein that man is laid.

There's one that in the church-yard lies
　For whom the bell did toll;
He lies in consecrated ground,
But for all the wealth in Bristol town
　I would not be with his soul!

Did'st see a house below the hill
　That the winds and the rains destroy?
'Twas then a farm where he did dwell,
And I remember it full well
　When I was a growing boy.

And she was a poor parish girl
　That came up from the west,
From service hard she ran away
And at that house in evil day
　Was taken in to rest.

The man he was a wicked man
　And an evil life he led;
Rage made his cheek grow deadly white
And his grey eyes were large and light,
　And in anger they grew red.

The man was bad, the mother worse,
　Bad fruit of a bad stem,
'Twould make your hair to stand-on-end
If I should tell to you my friend
　The things that were told of them!

Did'st see an out-house standing by?
　The walls alone remain;
It was a stable then, but now
Its mossy roof has fallen through
　All rotted by the rain.

The poor girl she had serv'd with them
　Some half-a-year, or more,
When she was found hung up one day
Stiff as a corpse and cold as clay
　Behind that stable door!

It is a very lonesome place,
  No hut or house is near;
Should one meet a murderer there alone
'Twere vain to scream, and the dying groan
  Would never reach mortal ear.

And there were strange reports about
  That the coroner never guest.
So he decreed that she should lie
Where four roads meet in infamy,
  With a stake drove in her breast.

Upon a board they carried her
  To the place where four roads met,
And I was one among the throng
That hither followed them along,
  I shall never the sight forget!

They carried her upon a board
  In the cloaths in which she died;
I saw the cap blow off her head,
Her face was of a dark dark red
  Her eyes were starting wide:

I think they could not have been closed
  So widely did they strain.
I never saw so dreadful a sight,
And it often made me wake at night,
  For I saw her face again.

They laid her here where four roads meet.
  Beneath this very place,
The earth upon her corpse was prest,
This post is driven into her breast,
  And a stone is on her face.

THE SAILOR
WHO HAD SERVED IN THE SLAVE TRADE

In September, 1798, a Dissenting Minister of Bristol, discovered a Sailor in the neighbourhood of that City, groaning and praying in a hovel. The circumstance that occasioned his agony of mind is detailed in the annexed Ballad, without the slightest addition or alteration. By presenting it as a Poem the story is made more public, and such stories ought to be made as public as possible.

The Sailor, Who Had Served In The Slave-Trade.

> He stopt,--it surely was a groan
>   That from the hovel came!
> He stopt and listened anxiously
>   Again it sounds the same.
>
> It surely from the hovel comes!
>   And now he hastens there,
> And thence he hears the name of Christ
>   Amidst a broken prayer.
>
> He entered in the hovel now,
>   A sailor there he sees,
> His hands were lifted up to Heaven
>   And he was on his knees.
>
> Nor did the Sailor so intent
>   His entering footsteps heed,
> But now the Lord's prayer said, and now
>   His half-forgotten creed.
>
> And often on his Saviour call'd
>   With many a bitter groan,
> In such heart-anguish as could spring
>   From deepest guilt alone.
>
> He ask'd the miserable man
>   Why he was kneeling there,
> And what the crime had been that caus'd
>   The anguish of his prayer.

Oh I have done a wicked thing!
　It haunts me night and day,
And I have sought this lonely place
　Here undisturb'd to pray.

I have no place to pray on board
　So I came here alone,
That I might freely kneel and pray,
　And call on Christ and groan.

If to the main-mast head I go,
　The wicked one is there,
From place to place, from rope to rope,
　He follows every where.

I shut my eyes,--it matters not--
　Still still the same I see,--
And when I lie me down at night
　'Tis always day with me.

He follows follows every where,
　And every place is Hell!
O God--and I must go with him
　In endless fire to dwell.

He follows follows every where,
　He's still above--below,
Oh tell me where to fly from him!
　Oh tell me where to go!

But tell me, quoth the Stranger then,
　What this thy crime hath been,
So haply I may comfort give
　To one that grieves for sin.

O I have done a cursed deed
　The wretched man replies,
And night and day and every where
　'Tis still before my eyes.

I sail'd on board a Guinea-man
　And to the slave-coast went;
Would that the sea had swallowed me
　When I was innocent!

And we took in our cargo there,
  Three hundred negroe slaves,
And we sail'd homeward merrily
  Over the ocean waves.

But some were sulky of the slaves
  And would not touch their meat,
So therefore we were forced by threats
  And blows to make them eat.

One woman sulkier than the rest
  Would still refuse her food,--
O Jesus God! I hear her cries--
  I see her in her blood!

The Captain made me tie her up
  And flog while he stood by,
And then he curs'd me if I staid
  My hand to hear her cry.

She groan'd, she shriek'd--I could not spare
  For the Captain he stood by--
Dear God! that I might rest one night
  From that poor woman's cry!

She twisted from the blows--her blood
  Her mangled flesh I see--
And still the Captain would not spare--
  Oh he was worse than me!

She could not be more glad than I
  When she was taken down,
A blessed minute--'twas the last
  That I have ever known!

I did not close my eyes all night,
  Thinking what I had done;
I heard her groans and they grew faint
  About the rising sun.

She groan'd and groan'd, but her groans grew
  Fainter at morning tide,
Fainter and fainter still they came
  Till at the noon she died.

They flung her overboard;--poor wretch
  She rested from her pain,--
But when--O Christ! O blessed God!
  Shall I have rest again!

I saw the sea close over her,
  Yet she was still in sight;
I see her twisting every where;
  I see her day and night.

Go where I will, do what I can
  The wicked one I see--
Dear Christ have mercy on my soul,
  O God deliver me!

To morrow I set sail again
  Not to the Negroe shore--
Wretch that I am I will at least
  Commit that sin no more.

O give me comfort if you can--
  Oh tell me where to fly--
And bid me hope, if there be hope,
  For one so lost as I.

Poor wretch, the stranger he replied,
  Put thou thy trust in heaven,
And call on him for whose dear sake
  All sins shall be forgiven.

This night at least is thine, go thou
  And seek the house of prayer,
There shalt thou hear the word of God
  And he will help thee there!

JASPAR

THE stories of the two following ballads are wholly imaginary. I may say of each as John Bunyan did of his 'Pilgrim's Progress',

> "It came from mine own heart, so to my head,
> And thence into my fingers trickled;
> Then to my pen, from whence immediately
> On paper I did dribble it daintily."

Jaspar

Jaspar was poor, and want and vice
  Had made his heart like stone,
And Jaspar look'd with envious eyes
  On riches not his own.

On plunder bent abroad he went
  Towards the close of day,
And loiter'd on the lonely road
  Impatient for his prey.

No traveller came, he loiter'd long
  And often look'd around,
And paus'd and listen'd eagerly
  To catch some coming sound.

He sat him down beside the stream
  That crossed the lonely way,
So fair a scene might well have charm'd
  All evil thoughts away;

He sat beneath a willow tree
  That cast a trembling shade,
The gentle river full in front
  A little island made,

Where pleasantly the moon-beam shone
  Upon the poplar trees,
Whose shadow on the stream below
  Play'd slowly to the breeze.

He listen'd--and he heard the wind
  That waved the willow tree;
He heard the waters flow along
  And murmur quietly.

He listen'd for the traveller's tread,
  The nightingale sung sweet,--
He started up, for now he heard
  The sound of coming feet;

He started up and graspt a stake
  And waited for his prey;
There came a lonely traveller
  And Jaspar crost his way.

But Jaspar's threats and curses fail'd
  The traveller to appal,
He would not lightly yield the purse
  That held his little all.

Awhile he struggled, but he strove
  With Jaspar's strength in vain;
Beneath his blows he fell and groan'd,
  And never spoke again.

He lifted up the murdered man
  And plunged him in the flood,
And in the running waters then
  He cleansed his hands from blood.

The waters closed around the corpse
  And cleansed his hands from gore,
The willow waved, the stream flowed on
  And murmured as before.

There was no human eye had seen
  The blood the murderer spilt,
And Jaspar's conscience never knew
  The avenging goad of guilt.

And soon the ruffian had consum'd
  The gold he gain'd so ill,
And years of secret guilt pass'd on
  And he was needy still.

One eve beside the alehouse fire
  He sat as it befell,
When in there came a labouring man
  Whom Jaspar knew full well.

He sat him down by Jaspar's side
  A melancholy man,
For spite of honest toil, the world
  Went hard with Jonathan.

His toil a little earn'd, and he
  With little was content,
But sickness on his wife had fallen
  And all he had was spent.

Then with his wife and little ones
  He shared the scanty meal,
And saw their looks of wretchedness,
  And felt what wretches feel.

That very morn the Landlord's power
  Had seized the little left,
And now the sufferer found himself
  Of every thing bereft.

He lent his head upon his hand,
  His elbow on his knee,
And so by Jaspar's side he sat
  And not a word said he.

Nay--why so downcast? Jaspar cried,
  Come--cheer up Jonathan!
Drink neighbour drink! 'twill warm thy heart,
  Come! come! take courage man!

He took the cup that Jaspar gave
  And down he drain'd it quick
I have a wife, said Jonathan,
  And she is deadly sick.

She has no bed to lie upon,
  I saw them take her bed.
And I have children--would to God
  That they and I were dead!

Our Landlord he goes home to night
  And he will sleep in peace.
I would that I were in my grave
  For there all troubles cease.

In vain I pray'd him to forbear
  Tho' wealth enough has he--
God be to him as merciless
  As he has been to me!

When Jaspar saw the poor man's soul
  On all his ills intent,
He plied him with the heartening cup
  And with him forth he went.

This landlord on his homeward road
  'Twere easy now to meet.
The road is lonesome--Jonathan,
  And vengeance, man! is sweet.

He listen'd to the tempter's voice
  The thought it made him start.
His head was hot, and wretchedness
  Had hardened now his heart.

Along the lonely road they went
  And waited for their prey,
They sat them down beside the stream
  That crossed the lonely way.

They sat them down beside the stream
  And never a word they said,
They sat and listen'd silently
  To hear the traveller's tread.

The night was calm, the night was dark,
  No star was in the sky,
The wind it waved the willow boughs,
  The stream flowed quietly.

The night was calm, the air was still,
  Sweet sung the nightingale,
The soul of Jonathan was sooth'd,
  His heart began to fail.

'Tis weary waiting here, he cried,
  And now the hour is late,--
Methinks he will not come to night,
  'Tis useless more to wait.

Have patience man! the ruffian said,
  A little we may wait,
But longer shall his wife expect
  Her husband at the gate.

Then Jonathan grew sick at heart,
  My conscience yet is clear,
Jaspar--it is not yet too late--
  I will not linger here.

How now! cried Jaspar, why I thought
  Thy conscience was asleep.
No more such qualms, the night is dark,
  The river here is deep,

What matters that, said Jonathan,
  Whose blood began to freeze,
When there is one above whose eye
  The deeds of darkness sees?

We are safe enough, said Jaspar then
  If that be all thy fear;
Nor eye below, nor eye above
  Can pierce the darkness here.

That instant as the murderer spake
  There came a sudden light;
Strong as the mid-day sun it shone,
  Though all around was night.

It hung upon the willow tree,
  It hung upon the flood,
It gave to view the poplar isle
  And all the scene of blood.

The traveller who journies there
  He surely has espied
A madman who has made his home
  Upon the river's side.

His cheek is pale, his eye is wild,
  His look bespeaks despair;
For Jaspar since that hour has made
  His home unshelter'd there.

And fearful are his dreams at night
  And dread to him the day;
He thinks upon his untold crime
  And never dares to pray.

The summer suns, the winter storms,
  O'er him unheeded roll,
For heavy is the weight of blood
  Upon the maniac's soul.

LORD WILLIAM

No eye beheld when William plunged
  Young Edmund in the stream,
No human ear but William's heard
  Young Edmund's drowning scream.

Submissive all the vassals own'd
  The murderer for their Lord,
And he, the rightful heir, possessed
  The house of Erlingford.

The ancient house of Erlingford
  Stood midst a fair domain,
And Severn's ample waters near
  Roll'd through the fertile plain.

And often the way-faring man
  Would love to linger there,
Forgetful of his onward road
  To gaze on scenes so fair.

But never could Lord William dare
  To gaze on Severn's stream;
In every wind that swept its waves
  He heard young Edmund scream.

In vain at midnight's silent hour
  Sleep closed the murderer's eyes,
In every dream the murderer saw
  Young Edmund's form arise.

In vain by restless conscience driven
  Lord William left his home,
Far from the scenes that saw his guilt,
  In pilgrimage to roam.

To other climes the pilgrim fled,
  But could not fly despair,
He sought his home again, but peace
  Was still a stranger there.

Each hour was tedious long, yet swift
  The months appear'd to roll;
And now the day return'd that shook
  With terror William's soul.

A day that William never felt
  Return without dismay,
For well had conscience kalendered
  Young Edmund's dying day.

A fearful day was that! the rains
  Fell fast, with tempest roar,
And the swoln tide of Severn spread
  Far on the level shore.

In vain Lord William sought the feast
  In vain he quaff'd the bowl,
And strove with noisy mirth to drown
  The anguish of his soul.

The tempest as its sudden swell
  In gusty howlings came,
With cold and death-like feelings seem'd
  To thrill his shuddering frame.

Reluctant now, as night came on,
  His lonely couch he prest,
And wearied out, he sunk to sleep,
  To sleep, but not to rest.

Beside that couch his brother's form
  Lord Edmund seem'd to stand,
Such and so pale as when in death
  He grasp'd his brother's hand;

Such and so pale his face as when
  With faint and faltering tongue,
To William's care, a dying charge
  He left his orphan son.

"I bade thee with a father's love
  My orphan Edmund guard--
Well William hast thou kept thy charge!
  Now take thy due reward."

He started up, each limb convuls'd
  With agonizing fear,
He only heard the storm of night--
  'Twas music to his ear.

When lo! the voice of loud alarm
  His inmost soul appals,
What ho! Lord William rise in haste!
  The water saps thy walls!

He rose in haste, beneath the walls
  He saw the flood appear,
It hemm'd him round, 'twas midnight now,
  No human aid was near.

He heard the shout of joy, for now
  A boat approach'd the wall,
And eager to the welcome aid
  They crowd for safety all.

My boat is small, the boatman cried,
  This dangerous haste forbear!
Wait other aid, this little bark
  But one from hence can bear.

Lord William leap'd into the boat,
  Haste--haste to yonder shore!
And ample wealth shall well reward,
  Ply swift and strong the oar.

The boatman plied the oar, the boat
  Went light along the stream,
Sudden Lord William heard a cry
  Like Edmund's drowning scream.

The boatman paus'd, methought I heard
  A child's distressful cry!
'Twas but the howling wind of night
  Lord William made reply.

Haste haste--ply swift and strong the oar!
  Haste haste across the stream!
Again Lord William heard a cry
  Like Edmund's drowning scream.

I heard a child's distressful scream
  The boatman cried again.
Nay hasten on--the night is dark--
  And we should search in vain.

Oh God! Lord William dost thou know
  How dreadful 'tis to die?
And can'st thou without pity hear
  A child's expiring cry?

How horrible it is to sink
  Beneath the chilly stream,
To stretch the powerless arms in vain,
  In vain for help to scream?

The shriek again was heard. It came
  More deep, more piercing loud,
That instant o'er the flood the moon
  Shone through a broken cloud.

And near them they beheld a child,
  Upon a crag he stood,
A little crag, and all around
  Was spread the rising flood.

The boatman plied the oar, the boat
  Approach'd his resting place,
The moon-beam shone upon the child
  And show'd how pale his face.

Now reach thine hand! the boatman cried
  Lord William reach and save!
The child stretch'd forth his little hands
  To grasp the hand he gave.

Then William shriek'd; the hand he touch'd
  Was cold and damp and dead!
He felt young Edmund in his arms
  A heavier weight than lead.

The boat sunk down, the murderer sunk
  Beneath the avenging stream;
He rose, he scream'd, no human ear
  Heard William's drowning scream.

A BALLAD
SHEWING HOW AN OLD WOMAN RODE DOUBLE
AND WHO RODE BEFORE HER.

A.D. 852. Circa dies istos, mulier quaedam malefica, in villa quae Berkeleia dicitur degens, gulae amatrix ac petulantiae, flagitiis modum usque in senium et auguriis non ponens, usque ad mortem impudica permansit. Haec die quadam cum sederet ad prandium, cornicula quam pro delitiis pascebat, nescio quid garrire coepit; quo audito, mulieris cultellus de manu excidit, simul et facies pallescere coepit, et emisso rugitu, hodie, inquit, accipiam grande incommodum, hodieque ad sulcum ultimum meum pervenit aratrum, quo dicto, nuncius doloris intravit; muliere vero percunctata ad quid veniret, affero, inquit, tibi filii tui obitum & totius familiae ejus ex subita ruina interitum. Hoc quoque dolore mulier permota, lecto protinus decubuit graviter infirmata; sentiensque morbum subrepere ad vitalia, liberos quos habuit superstites, monachum videlicet et monacham, per epistolam invitavit; advenientes autem voce singultiente alloquitur. Ego, inquit, o pueri, meo miserabili fato daemoniacis semper artibus inservivi; ego omnium vitiorum sentina, ego illecebrarum omnium fui magistra. Erat tamen mihi inter haec mala, spes vestrae religionis, quae meam solidaret animam desperatam; vos expctabam propugnatores contra daemones, tutores contra saevissimos hostes. Nunc igitur quoniam ad finem vitae perveni, rogo vos per materna ubera, ut mea tentatis alleviare tormenta. Insuite me defunctam in corio cervino, ac deinde in sarcophago lapideo supponite, operculumque ferro et plumbo constringite, ac demum lapidem tribus cathenis ferreis et fortissimis circundantes, clericos quinquaginta psalmorum cantores, et tot per tres dies presbyteros missarum celebratores applicate, qui feroces lenigent adversariorum incursus. Ita si tribus noctibus secura jacuero, quarta die me infodite humo.

Factumque est ut praeceperat illis. Sed, proh dolor! nil preces, nil lacrymae, nil demum valuere catenae. Primis enim duabus noctibus, cum chori psallentium corpori assistabant, advenientes Daemones ostium ecclesiae confregerunt ingenti obice clausum, extremasque cathenas negotio levi dirumpunt: media autem quae fortior erat, illibata manebat. Tertia autem nocte, circa gallicinium, strepitu hostium adventantium, omne monasterium visum est a fundamento moveri. Unus ergo daemonum, et vultu caeteris terribilior & statura eminentior, januas Ecclesiae; impetu violento concussas in fragmenta dejecit. Divexerunt clerici cum laicis, metu stelerunt omnium capilli, et psalmorum concentus defecit. Daemon ergo gestu ut videbatur arroganti ad sepulchrum accedens, & nomen mulieris modicum ingeminans, surgere imperavit. Qua respondente, quod nequiret pro vinculis, jam malo tuo, inquit, solveris; et protinus cathenam quae caeterorum ferociam daemonum deluserat, velut stuppeum vinculum rumpebat. Operculum etiam sepulchri pede depellens, mulierem palam omnibus ab ecclesia extraxit, ubi prae foribus niger equus superbe hinniens videbatur, uncis ferreis et clavis undique confixus, super quem misera mulier projecta, ab oculis assistentium evanuit. Audiebantur tamen clamores per quatuor fere miliaria horribiles, auxilium postulantes.

Ista itaque quae retuli incredibilia non erunt, si legatur beati Gregorii dialogus, in quo refert, hominem in ecclesia sepultam, a daemonibus foras ejectum. Et apud Francos Carolus Martellus insignis vir fortudinis, qui Saracenos Galliam ingressos, Hispaniam redire compulit, exactis vitae suae diebus, in Ecclesia beati Dionysii legitur fuisse sepultus. Sed quia patrimonia, cum decimis omnium fere ecclesiarum Galliae, pro stipendio commilitonum suorum mutilaverat, miserabiliter a malignis spiritibus de sepulchro corporaliter avulsus, usque in hodiernum diem nusquamcomparuit.

Matthew of Westminster.

This story is also related by Olaus Magnus, and in the Nuremberg Chronicle, from which the wooden cut is taken.

A Ballad, Shewing How An Old Woman Rode Double, And Who Rode Before Her.

> The Raven croak'd as she sate at her meal,
>   And the Old Woman knew what he said,
> And she grew pale at the Raven's tale,
>   And sicken'd and went to her bed.
>
> Now fetch me my children, and fetch them with speed,
>   The Old Woman of Berkeley said,
> The monk my son, and my daughter the nun,
>   Bid them hasten or I shall be dead.
>
> The monk her son, and her daughter the nun,
>   Their way to Berkeley went,
> And they have brought with pious thought
>   The holy sacrament.
>
> The old Woman shriek'd as they entered her door,
>   'Twas fearful her shrieks to hear,
> Now take the sacrament away
>   For mercy, my children dear!
>
> Her lip it trembled with agony,
>   The sweat ran down her brow,
> I have tortures in store for evermore,
>   Oh! spare me my children now!
>
> Away they sent the sacrament,
>   The fit it left her weak,
> She look'd at her children with ghastly eyes
>   And faintly struggled to speak.

All kind of sin I have rioted in
　And the judgment now must be,
But I secured my childrens souls,
　Oh! pray my children for me.

I have suck'd the breath of sleeping babes,
　The fiends have been my slaves,
I have nointed myself with infants fat,
　And feasted on rifled graves.

And the fiend will fetch me now in fire
　My witchcrafts to atone,
And I who have rifled the dead man's grave
　Shall never have rest in my own.

Bless I intreat my winding sheet
　My children I beg of you!
And with holy water sprinkle my shroud
　And sprinkle my coffin too.

And let me be chain'd in my coffin of stone
　And fasten it strong I implore
With iron bars, and let it be chain'd
　With three chains to the church floor.

And bless the chains and sprinkle them,
　And let fifty priests stand round,
Who night and day the mass may say
　Where I lie on the ground.

And let fifty choristers be there
　The funeral dirge to sing,
Who day and night by the taper's light
　Their aid to me may bring.

Let the church bells all both great and small
　Be toll'd by night and day,
To drive from thence the fiends who come
　To bear my corpse away.

And ever have the church door barr'd
　After the even song,
And I beseech you children dear
　Let the bars and bolts be strong.

And let this be three days and nights
  My wretched corpse to save,
Preserve me so long from the fiendish throng
  And then I may rest in my grave.

The Old Woman of Berkeley laid her down
  And her eyes grew deadly dim,
Short came her breath and the struggle of death
  Did loosen every limb.

They blest the old woman's winding sheet
  With rites and prayers as due,
With holy water they sprinkled her shroud
  And they sprinkled her coffin too.

And they chain'd her in her coffin of stone
  And with iron barr'd it down,
And in the church with three strong chains
  They chain'd it to the ground.

And they blest the chains and sprinkled them,
  And fifty priests stood round,
By night and day the mass to say
  Where she lay on the ground.

And fifty choristers were there
  To sing the funeral song,
And a hallowed taper blazed in the hand
  Of all the sacred throng.

To see the priests and choristers
  It was a goodly sight,
Each holding, as it were a staff,
  A taper burning bright.

And the church bells all both great and small
  Did toll so loud and long,
And they have barr'd the church door hard
  After the even song.

And the first night the taper's light
  Burnt steadily and clear.
But they without a hideous rout
  Of angry fiends could hear;

A hideous roar at the church door
  Like a long thunder peal,
And the priests they pray'd and the choristers sung
  Louder in fearful zeal.

Loud toll'd the bell, the priests pray'd well,
  The tapers they burnt bright,
The monk her son, and her daughter the nun
  They told their beads all night.

The cock he crew, away they flew
  The fiends from the herald of day,
And undisturb'd the choristers sing
  And the fifty priests they pray.

The second night the taper's light
  Burnt dismally and blue,
And every one saw his neighbour's face
  Like a dead man's face to view.

And yells and cries without arise
  That the stoutest heart might shock,
And a deafening roaring like a cataract pouring
  Over a mountain rock.

The monk and nun they told their beads
  As fast as they could tell,
And aye as louder grew the noise
  The faster went the bell.

Louder and louder the choristers sung
  As they trembled more and more,
And the fifty priests prayed to heaven for aid,
  They never had prayed so before.

The cock he crew, away they flew
  The fiends from the herald of day,
And undisturb'd the choristers sing
  And the fifty priests they pray.

The third night came and the tapers flame
  A hideous stench did make,
And they burnt as though they had been dipt
  In the burning brimstone lake.

And the loud commotion, like the rushing of ocean,
  Grew momently more and more,
And strokes as of a battering ram
  Did shake the strong church door.

The bellmen they for very fear
  Could toll the bell no longer,
And still as louder grew the strokes
  Their fear it grew the stronger.

The monk and nun forgot their beads,
  They fell on the ground dismay'd,
There was not a single saint in heaven
  Whom they did not call to aid.

And the choristers song that late was so strong
  Grew a quaver of consternation,
For the church did rock as an earthquake shock
  Uplifted its foundation.

And a sound was heard like the trumpet's blast
  That shall one day wake the dead,
The strong church door could bear no more
  And the bolts and the bars they fled.

And the taper's light was extinguish'd quite,
  And the choristers faintly sung,
And the priests dismay'd, panted and prayed
  Till fear froze every tongue.

And in He came with eyes of flame
  The Fiend to fetch the dead,
And all the church with his presence glowed
  Like a fiery furnace red.

He laid his hand on the iron chains
  And like flax they moulder'd asunder,
And the coffin lid that was barr'd so firm
  He burst with his voice of thunder.

And he bade the Old Woman of Berkeley rise
  And come with her master away,
And the cold sweat stood on the cold cold corpse,
  At the voice she was forced to obey.

She rose on her feet in her winding sheet,
  Her dead flesh quivered with fear,
And a groan like that which the Old Woman gave
  Never did mortal hear.

She followed the fiend to the church door,
  There stood a black horse there,
His breath was red like furnace smoke,
  His eyes like a meteor's glare.

The fiendish force flung her on the horse
  And he leapt up before,
And away like the lightning's speed they went
  And she was seen no more.

They saw her no more, but her cries and shrieks
  For four miles round they could hear,
And children at rest at their mother's breast,
  Started and screamed with fear.

THE SURGEON'S WARNING

THE subject of this parody was given me by a friend, to whom also I am indebted for some of the stanzas.

Respecting the patent coffins herein mentioned, after the manner of Catholic Poets, who confess the actions they attribute to their Saints and Deity to be but fiction, I hereby declare that it is by no means my design to depreciate that useful invention; and all persons to whom this Ballad shall come are requested to take notice, that nothing here asserted concerning the aforesaid Coffins is true, except that the maker and patentee lives by St. Martin's Lane.

The Surgeons' Warning.

> The Doctor whispered to the Nurse
>   And the Surgeon knew what he said,
> And he grew pale at the Doctor's tale
>   And trembled in his sick bed.
>
> Now fetch me my brethren and fetch them with speed
>   The Surgeon affrighted said,
> The Parson and the Undertaker,
>   Let them hasten or I shall be dead.
>
> The Parson and the Undertaker
>   They hastily came complying,
> And the Surgeon's Prentices ran up stairs
>   When they heard that their master was dying.
>
> The Prentices all they entered the room
>   By one, by two, by three,
> With a sly grin came Joseph in,
>   First of the company.
>
> The Surgeon swore as they enter'd his door,
>   'Twas fearful his oaths to hear,--
> Now send these scoundrels to the Devil,
>   For God's sake my brethren dear.
>
> He foam'd at the mouth with the rage he felt
>   And he wrinkled his black eye-brow,
> That rascal Joe would be at me I know,
>   But zounds let him spare me now.
>
> Then out they sent the Prentices,
>   The fit it left him weak,

He look'd at his brothers with ghastly eyes,
  And faintly struggled to speak.

All kinds of carcasses I have cut up,
  And the judgment now must be--
But brothers I took care of you,
  So pray take care of me!

I have made candles of infants fat
  The Sextons have been my slaves,
I have bottled babes unborn, and dried
  Hearts and livers from rifled graves.

And my Prentices now will surely come
  And carve me bone from bone,
And I who have rifled the dead man's grave
  Shall never have rest in my own.

Bury me in lead when I am dead,
  My brethren I intreat,
And see the coffin weigh'd I beg
  Lest the Plumber should be a cheat.

And let it be solder'd closely down
  Strong as strong can be I implore,
And put it in a patent coffin,
  That I may rise no more.

If they carry me off in the patent coffin
  Their labour will be in vain,
Let the Undertaker see it bought of the maker
  Who lives by St. Martin's lane.

And bury me in my brother's church
  For that will safer be,
And I implore lock the church door
  And pray take care of the key.

And all night long let three stout men
  The vestry watch within,
To each man give a gallon of beer
  And a keg of Holland's gin;

Powder and ball and blunder-buss
  To save me if he can,

And eke five guineas if he shoot
  A resurrection man.

And let them watch me for three weeks
  My wretched corpse to save,
For then I think that I may stink
  Enough to rest in my grave.

The Surgeon laid him down in his bed,
  His eyes grew deadly dim,
Short came his breath and the struggle of death
  Distorted every limb.

They put him in lead when he was dead
  And shrouded up so neat,
And they the leaden coffin weigh
  Lest the Plumber should be a cheat.

They had it solder'd closely down
  And examined it o'er and o'er,
And they put it in a patent coffin
  That he might rise no more.

For to carry him off in a patent coffin
  Would they thought be but labour in vain,
So the Undertaker saw it bought of the maker
  Who lives by St. Martin's lane.

In his brother's church they buried him
  That safer he might be,
They lock'd the door and would not trust
  The Sexton with the key.

And three men in the vestry watch
  To save him if they can,
And should he come there to shoot they swear
  A resurrection man.

And the first night by lanthorn light
  Thro' the church-yard as they went,
A guinea of gold the sexton shewed
  That Mister Joseph sent.

But conscience was tough, it was not enough
  And their honesty never swerved,

And they bade him go with Mister Joe
  To the Devil as he deserved.

So all night long by the vestry fire
  They quaff'd their gin and ale,
And they did drink as you may think
  And told full many a tale.

The second night by lanthorn light
  Thro' the church-yard as they went,
He whisper'd anew and shew'd them two
  That Mister Joseph sent.

The guineas were bright and attracted their sight
  They look'd so heavy and new,
And their fingers itch'd as they were bewitch'd
  And they knew not what to do.

But they waver'd not long for conscience was strong
  And they thought they might get more,
And they refused the gold, but not
  So rudely as before.

So all night long by the vestry fire
  They quaff'd their gin and ale,
And they did drink as you may think
  And told full many a tale.

The third night as by lanthorn light
  Thro' the church-yard they went,
He bade them see and shew'd them three
  That Mister Joseph sent.

They look'd askance with eager glance,
  The guineas they shone bright,
For the Sexton on the yellow gold
  Let fall his lanthorn light.

And he look'd sly with his roguish eye
  And gave a well-tim'd wink,
And they could not stand the sound in his hand
  For he made the guineas chink.

And conscience late that had such weight,
  All in a moment fails,

For well they knew that it was true
  A dead man told no tales,

And they gave all their powder and ball
  And took the gold so bright,
And they drank their beer and made good cheer,
  Till now it was midnight.

Then, tho' the key of the church door
  Was left with the Parson his brother,
It opened at the Sexton's touch--
  Because he had another.

And in they go with that villain Joe
  To fetch the body by night,
And all the church look'd dismally
  By his dark lanthorn light.

They laid the pick-axe to the stones
  And they moved them soon asunder.
They shovell'd away the hard-prest clay
  And came to the coffin under.

They burst the patent coffin first
  And they cut thro' the lead,
And they laugh'd aloud when they saw the shroud
  Because they had got at the dead.

And they allowed the Sexton the shroud
  And they put the coffin back,
And nose and knees they then did squeeze
  The Surgeon in a sack.

The watchmen as they past along
  Full four yards off could smell,
And a curse bestowed upon the load
  So disagreeable.

So they carried the sack a-pick-a-back
  And they carv'd him bone from bone,
But what became of the Surgeon's soul
  Was never to mortal known.

THE VICTORY

Hark--how the church-bells thundering harmony
Stuns the glad ear! tidings of joy have come,
Good tidings of great joy! two gallant ships
Met on the element,--they met, they fought
A desperate fight!--good tidings of great joy!
Old England triumphed! yet another day
Of glory for the ruler of the waves!
For those who fell, 'twas in their country's cause,
They have their passing paragraphs of praise
And are forgotten.
  There was one who died
In that day's glory, whose obscurer name
No proud historian's page will chronicle.
Peace to his honest soul! I read his name,
'Twas in the list of slaughter, and blest God
The sound was not familiar to mine ear.
But it was told me after that this man
Was one whom lawful violence [1] had forced
From his own home and wife and little ones,
Who by his labour lived; that he was one
Whose uncorrupted heart could keenly feel
A husband's love, a father's anxiousness,
That from the wages of his toil he fed
The distant dear ones, and would talk of them
At midnight when he trod the silent deck
With him he valued, talk of them, of joys
That he had known--oh God! and of the hour
When they should meet again, till his full heart
His manly heart at last would overflow
Even like a child's with very tenderness.
Peace to his honest spirit! suddenly
It came, and merciful the ball of death,
For it came suddenly and shattered him,
And left no moment's agonizing thought
On those he loved so well.
          He ocean deep
Now lies at rest. Be Thou her comforter
Who art the widow's friend! Man does not know
What a cold sickness made her blood run back
When first she heard the tidings of the fight;
Man does not know with what a dreadful hope
She listened to the names of those who died,
Man does not know, or knowing will not heed,

With what an agony of tenderness
She gazed upon her children, and beheld
His image who was gone. Oh God! be thou
Her comforter who art the widow's friend!

1: The person alluded to was pressed into the service.

HENRY THE HERMIT

It was a little island where he dwelt,
Or rather a lone rock, barren and bleak,
Short scanty herbage spotting with dark spots
Its gray stone surface. Never mariner
Approach'd that rude and uninviting coast,
Nor ever fisherman his lonely bark
Anchored beside its shore. It was a place
Befitting well a rigid anchoret,
Dead to the hopes, and vanities, and joys
And purposes of life; and he had dwelt
Many long years upon that lonely isle,
For in ripe manhood he abandoned arms,
Honours and friends and country and the world,
And had grown old in solitude. That isle
Some solitary man in other times
Had made his dwelling-place; and Henry found
The little chapel that his toil had built
Now by the storms unroofed, his bed of leaves
Wind-scattered, and his grave o'ergrown with grass,
And thistles, whose white seeds winged in vain
Withered on rocks, or in the waves were lost.
So he repaired the chapel's ruined roof,
Clear'd the grey lichens from the altar-stone,
And underneath a rock that shelter'd him
From the sea blasts, he built his hermitage.

The peasants from the shore would bring him food
And beg his prayers; but human converse else
He knew not in that utter solitude,
Nor ever visited the haunts of men
Save when some sinful wretch on a sick bed
Implored his blessing and his aid in death.
That summons he delayed not to obey,
Tho' the night tempest or autumnal wind.
Maddened the waves, and tho' the mariner,
Albeit relying on his saintly load,
Grew pale to see the peril. So he lived
A most austere and self-denying man,
Till abstinence, and age, and watchfulness
Exhausted him, and it was pain at last
To rise at midnight from his bed of leaves
And bend his knees in prayer. Yet not the less
Tho' with reluctance of infirmity,

He rose at midnight from his bed of leaves
And bent his knees in prayer; but with more zeal
More self-condemning fervour rais'd his voice
For pardon for that sin, 'till that the sin
Repented was a joy like a good deed.

One night upon the shore his chapel bell
Was heard; the air was calm, and its far sounds
Over the water came distinct and loud.
Alarmed at that unusual hour to hear
Its toll irregular, a monk arose.
The boatmen bore him willingly across
For well the hermit Henry was beloved.
He hastened to the chapel, on a stone
Henry was sitting there, cold, stiff and dead,
The bell-rope in his band, and at his feet
The lamp that stream'd a long unsteady light

1: This story is related in the English Martyrology, 1608.

ENGLISH ECLOGUES

THE following Eclogues I believe, bear no resemblance to any poems in our language. This species of composition has become popular in Germany, and I was induced to attempt by an account of the German Idylls given me in conversation. They cannot properly be stiled imitations, as I am ignorant of that language at present, and have never seen any translations or specimens in this kind.

With bad Eclogues I am sufficiently acquainted, from ??tyrus [1] and Corydon down to our English Strephons and Thirsises. No kind of poetry can boast of more illustrious names or is more distinguished by the servile dulness of imitated nonsense. Pastoral writers "more silly than their sheep" have like their sheep gone on in the same track one after another. Gay stumbled into a new path. His eclogues were the only ones that interested me when I was a boy, and did not know they were burlesque. The subject would furnish matter for a long essay, but thisis not the place for it.

How far poems requiring almost a colloquial plainness of language may accord with the public taste I am doubtful. They have been subjected to able criticism and revised with care. I have endeavoured to make them true to nature.

1: The letters of this name are illegible (worn away?) in the original text; from the remaining bits I have guessed all but the first two, which are not visible under any magnification. text Ed.

ECLOGUE I

THE OLD MANSION-HOUSE

STRANGER.
>Old friend! why you seem bent on parish duty,
>Breaking the highway stones,--and 'tis a task
>Somewhat too hard methinks for age like yours.

OLD MAN.
>Why yes! for one with such a weight of years
>Upon his back. I've lived here, man and boy,
>In this same parish, near the age of man
>For I am hard upon threescore and ten.
>I can remember sixty years ago
>The beautifying of this mansion here
>When my late Lady's father, the old Squire
>Came to the estate.

STRANGER.
>>Why then you have outlasted
>All his improvements, for you see they're making
>Great alterations here.

OLD MAN.
>>Aye-great indeed!
>And if my poor old Lady could rise up--
>God rest her soul! 'twould grieve her to behold
>The wicked work is here.

STRANGER.
>>They've set about it
>In right good earnest. All the front is gone,
>Here's to be turf they tell me, and a road
>Round to the door. There were some yew trees too
>Stood in the court.

OLD MAN.
>Aye Master! fine old trees!
>My grandfather could just remember back

When they were planted there. It was my task
To keep them trimm'd, and 'twas a pleasure to me!
All strait and smooth, and like a great green wall!
My poor old Lady many a time would come
And tell me where to shear, for she had played
In childhood under them, and 'twas her pride
To keep them in their beauty. Plague I say
On their new-fangled whimsies! we shall have
A modern shrubbery here stuck full of firs
And your pert poplar trees;--I could as soon
Have plough'd my father's grave as cut them down!

STRANGER.
    But 'twill be lighter and more chearful now,
A fine smooth turf, and with a gravel road
Round for the carriage,--now it suits my taste.
I like a shrubbery too, it looks so fresh,
And then there's some variety about it.
In spring the lilac and the gueldres rose,
And the laburnum with its golden flowers
Waving in the wind. And when the autumn comes
The bright red berries of the mountain ash,
With firs enough in winter to look green,
And show that something lives. Sure this is better
Than a great hedge of yew that makes it look
All the year round like winter, and for ever
Dropping its poisonous leaves from the under boughs
So dry and bare!

OLD MAN.
    Ah! so the new Squire thinks
And pretty work he makes of it! what 'tis
To have a stranger come to an old house!

STRANGER.

It seems you know him not?

OLD MAN.
    No Sir, not I.
They tell me he's expected daily now,

But in my Lady's time he never came
But once, for they were very distant kin.
If he had played about here when a child
In that fore court, and eat the yew-berries,
And sat in the porch threading the jessamine flowers,
That fell so thick, he had not had the heart
To mar all thus.

STRANGER.
    Come--come! all a not wrong.
    Those old dark windows--

OLD MAN.
        They're demolish'd too--
As if he could not see thro' casement glass!
The very red-breasts that so regular
Came to my Lady for her morning crumbs,
Won't know the window now!

STRANGER.
       Nay they were high
And then so darken'd up with jessamine,
Harbouring the vermine;--that was a fine tree
However. Did it not grow in and line
The porch?

OLD MAN.
    All over it: it did one good
To pass within ten yards when 'twas in blossom.
There was a sweet-briar too that grew beside.
My Lady loved at evening to sit there
And knit; and her old dog lay at her feet
And slept in the sun; 'twas an old favourite dog
She did not love him less that he was old
And feeble, and he always had a place
By the fire-side, and when he died at last
She made me dig a grave in the garden for him.
Ah I she was good to all! a woful day
'Twas for the poor when to her grave she went!

STRANGER.
>They lost a friend then?

OLD MAN.
>You're a stranger here
>Or would not ask that question. Were they sick?
>She had rare cordial waters, and for herbs
>She could have taught the Doctors. Then at winter
>When weekly she distributed the bread
>In the poor old porch, to see her and to hear
>The blessings on her! and I warrant them
>They were a blessing to her when her wealth
>Had been no comfort else. At Christmas, Sir!
>It would have warm'd your heart if you had seen
>Her Christmas kitchen,--how the blazing fire
>Made her fine pewter shine, and holly boughs
>So chearful red,--and as for misseltoe,
>The finest bough that grew in the country round
>Was mark'd for Madam. Then her old ale went
>So bountiful about! a Christmas cask,
>And 'twas a noble one! God help me Sir!
>But I shall never see such days again.

STRANGER.
>Things may be better yet than you suppose
>And you should hope the best.

OLD MAN.
>>It don't look well
>These alterations Sir! I'm an old man
>And love the good old fashions; we don't find
>Old bounty in new houses. They've destroyed
>All that my Lady loved; her favourite walk
>Grubb'd up, and they do say that the great row
>Of elms behind the house, that meet a-top
>They must fall too. Well! well! I did not think
>To live to see all this, and 'tis perhaps
>A comfort I shan't live to see it long.

STRANGER.
>But sure all changes are not needs for the worse

My friend.

OLD MAN.
    May-hap they mayn't Sir;--for all that
I like what I've been us'd to. I remember
All this from a child up, and now to lose it,
'Tis losing an old friend. There's nothing left
As 'twas;--I go abroad and only meet
With men whose fathers I remember boys;
The brook that used to run before my door
That's gone to the great pond; the trees I learnt
To climb are down; and I see nothing now
That tells me of old times, except the stones
In the church-yard. You are young Sir and I hope
Have many years in store,--but pray to God
You mayn't be left the last of all your friends.

STRANGER.
    Well! well! you've one friend more than you're aware of.
If the Squire's taste don't suit with your's, I warrant
That's all you'll quarrel with: walk in and taste
His beer, old friend! and see if your old Lady
E'er broached a better cask. You did not know me,
But we're acquainted now. 'Twould not be easy
To make you like the outside; but within--
That is not changed my friend! you'll always find
The same old bounty and old welcome there.

ECLOGUE II

THE GRANDMOTHERS TALE

JANE.
>Harry! I'm tired of playing. We'll draw round
>The fire, and Grandmamma perhaps will tell us
>One of her stories.

HARRY.
>Aye--dear Grandmamma!
>A pretty story! something dismal now;
>A bloody murder.

JANE.
>Or about a ghost.

GRANDMOTHER.
>Nay, nay, I should but frighten you. You know
>The other night when I was telling you
>About the light in the church-yard, how you trembled
>Because the screech-owl hooted at the window,
>And would not go to bed.

JANE.
>Why Grandmamma
>You said yourself you did not like to hear him.
>Pray now! we wo'nt be frightened.

GRANDMOTHER.
>Well, well, children!
>But you've heard all my stories. Let me see,--
>Did I never tell you how the smuggler murdered
>The woman down at Pill?

HARRY.
>No--never! never!

GRANDMOTHER.
   Not how he cut her head off in the stable?

HARRY.
   Oh--now! do tell us that!

GRANDMOTHER.
        You must have heard
Your Mother, children! often tell of her.
She used to weed in the garden here, and worm
Your uncle's dogs [1], and serve the house with coal;
And glad enough she was in winter time
To drive her asses here! it was cold work
To follow the slow beasts thro' sleet and snow,
And here she found a comfortable meal
And a brave fire to thaw her, for poor Moll
Was always welcome.

HARRY.
        Oh--'twas blear-eyed Moll
The collier woman,--a great ugly woman,
I've heard of her.

GRANDMOTHER.
        Ugly enough poor soul!
At ten yards distance you could hardly tell
If it were man or woman, for her voice
Was rough as our old mastiff's, and she wore
A man's old coat and hat,--and then her face!
There was a merry story told of her,
How when the press-gang came to take her husband
As they were both in bed, she heard them coming,
Drest John up in her night-cap, and herself
Put on his clothes and went before the Captain.

JANE.
   And so they prest a woman!

GRANDMOTHER.
>'Twas a trick
She dearly loved to tell, and all the country
Soon knew the jest, for she was used to travel
For miles around. All weathers and all hours
She crossed the hill, as hardy as her beasts,
Bearing the wind and rain and winter frosts,
And if she did not reach her home at night
She laid her down in the stable with her asses
And slept as sound as they did.

HARRY.
>With her asses!

GRANDMOTHER.
Yes, and she loved her beasts. For tho' poor wretch
She was a terrible reprobate and swore
Like any trooper, she was always good
To the dumb creatures, never loaded them
Beyond their strength, and rather I believe
Would stint herself than let the poor beasts want,
Because, she said, they could not ask for food.
I never saw her stick fall heavier on them
Than just with its own weight. She little thought
This tender-heartedness would be her death!
There was a fellow who had oftentimes,
As if he took delight in cruelty.
Ill-used her Asses. He was one who lived
By smuggling, and, for she had often met him
Crossing the down at night, she threatened him,
If he tormented them again, to inform
Of his unlawful ways. Well--so it was--
'Twas what they both were born to, he provoked her,
She laid an information, and one morn
They found her in the stable, her throat cut
From ear to ear,'till the head only hung
Just by a bit of skin.

JANE.
Oh dear! oh dear!

HARRY.
> I hope they hung the man!

GRANDMOTHER.
> They took him up;
> There was no proof, no one had seen the deed,
> And he was set at liberty. But God
> Whoss eye beholdeth all things, he had seen
> The murder, and the murderer knew that God
> Was witness to his crime. He fled the place,
> But nowhere could he fly the avenging hand
> Of heaven, but nowhere could the murderer rest,
> A guilty conscience haunted him, by day,
> By night, in company, in solitude,
> Restless and wretched, did he bear upon him
> The weight of blood; her cries were in his ears,
> Her stifled groans as when he knelt upon her
> Always he heard; always he saw her stand
> Before his eyes; even in the dead of night
> Distinctly seen as tho' in the broad sun,
> She stood beside the murderer's bed and yawn'd
> Her ghastly wound; till life itself became
> A punishment at last he could not bear,
> And he confess'd [2] it all, and gave himself
> To death, so terrible, he said, it was
> To have a guilty conscience!

HARRY.
> Was he hung then?

GRANDMOTHER.
> Hung and anatomized. Poor wretched man,
> Your uncles went to see him on his trial,
> He was so pale, so thin, so hollow-eyed,
> And such a horror in his meagre face,
> They said he look'd like one who never slept.
> He begg'd the prayers of all who saw his end
> And met his death with fears that well might warn
> From guilt, tho' not without a hope in Christ.

1: I know not whether this cruel and stupid custom is common in other parts of England. It is supposed to prevent the dogs from doing any mischief should they afterwards become mad.

2: There must be many persons living who remember these circumstances. They happened two or three and twenty years ago, in the neighbourhood of Bristol. The woman's name was Bees. The stratagem by which she preserved her husband from the press-gang, is also true.

ECLOGUE III

THE FUNERAL

The coffin [1] as I past across the lane
Came sudden on my view. It was not here,
A sight of every day, as in the streets
Of the great city, and we paus'd and ask'd
Who to the grave was going. It was one,
A village girl, they told us, who had borne
An eighteen months strange illness, and had pined
With such slow wasting that the hour of death
Came welcome to her. We pursued our way
To the house of mirth, and with that idle talk
That passes o'er the mind and is forgot,
We wore away the time. But it was eve
When homewardly I went, and in the air
Was that cool freshness, that discolouring shade
That makes the eye turn inward. Then I heard
Over the vale the heavy toll of death
Sound slow; it made me think upon the dead,
I questioned more and learnt her sorrowful tale.
She bore unhusbanded a mother's name,
And he who should have cherished her, far off
Sail'd on the seas, self-exil'd from his home,
For he was poor. Left thus, a wretched one,
Scorn made a mock of her, and evil tongues
Were busy with her name. She had one ill
Heavier, neglect, forgetfulness from him
Whom she had loved so dearly. Once he wrote,
But only once that drop of comfort came
To mingle with her cup of wretchedness;
And when his parents had some tidings from him,
There was no mention of poor Hannah there,
Or 'twas the cold enquiry, bitterer
Than silence. So she pined and pined away
And for herself and baby toil'd and toil'd,
Nor did she, even on her death bed, rest
From labour, knitting with her outstretch'd arms
Till she sunk with very weakness. Her old mother
Omitted no kind office, and she work'd
Hard, and with hardest working barely earn'd
Enough to make life struggle and prolong
The pains of grief and sickness. Thus she lay
On the sick bed of poverty, so worn

With her long suffering and that painful thought
That at her heart lay rankling, and so weak,
That she could make no effort to express
Affection for her infant; and the child,
Whose lisping love perhaps had solaced her
With a strange infantine ingratitude
Shunn'd her as one indifferent. She was past
That anguish, for she felt her hour draw on,
And 'twas her only comfort now to think
Upon the grave. "Poor girl!" her mother said,
"Thou hast suffered much!" "aye mother! there is none
"Can tell what I have suffered!" she replied,
"But I shall soon be where the weary rest."
And she did rest her soon, for it pleased God
To take her to his mercy.

1 It is proper to remark that the story related in this Eclogue is strictly true. I met the funeral, and learnt the circumstances in a village in Hampshire. The indifference of the child was mentioned to me; indeed no addition whatever has been made to the story. I should have thought it wrong to have weakened the effect of a faithful narrative by adding any thing.

ECLOGUE IV

THE SAILOR'S MOTHER

WOMAN.
    Sir for the love of God some small relief
    To a poor woman!

TRAVELLER.
    Whither are you bound?
    'Tis a late hour to travel o'er these downs,
    No house for miles around us, and the way
    Dreary and wild. The evening wind already
    Makes one's teeth chatter, and the very Sun,
    Setting so pale behind those thin white clouds,
    Looks cold. 'Twill be a bitter night!

WOMAN.
    Aye Sir
    'Tis cutting keen! I smart at every breath,
    Heaven knows how I shall reach my journey's end,
    For the way is long before me, and my feet,
    God help me! sore with travelling. I would gladly,
    If it pleased God, lie down at once and die.

TRAVELLER.
    Nay nay cheer up! a little food and rest
    Will comfort you; and then your journey's end
    Will make amends for all. You shake your head,
    And weep. Is it some evil business then
    That leads you from your home?

WOMAN.
        Sir I am going
    To see my son at Plymouth, sadly hurt
    In the late action, and in the hospital
    Dying, I fear me, now.

TRAVELLER.
        Perhaps your fears

                            Make evil worse. Even if a limb be lost
                            There may be still enough for comfort left
                            An arm or leg shot off, there's yet the heart
                            To keep life warm, and he may live to talk
                            With pleasure of the glorious fight that maim'd him,
                            Proud of his loss. Old England's gratitude
                            Makes the maim'd sailor happy.

WOMAN.
                                      'Tis not that--
                            An arm or leg--I could have borne with that.
                            'Twas not a ball, it was some cursed thing
                            That bursts [1] and burns that hurt him. Something Sir
                            They do not use on board our English ships
                            It is so wicked!

TRAVELLER.
                                Rascals! a mean art
                            Of cruel cowardice, yet all in vain!

WOMAN.
                            Yes Sir! and they should show no mercy to them
                            For making use of such unchristian arms.
                            I had a letter from the hospital,
                            He got some friend to write it, and he tells me
                            That my poor boy has lost his precious eyes,
                            Burnt out. Alas! that I should ever live
                            To see this wretched day!--they tell me Sir
                            There is no cure for wounds like his. Indeed
                            'Tis a hard journey that I go upon
                            To such a dismal end!

TRAVELLER.
                                He yet may live.
                            But if the worst should chance, why you must bear
                            The will of heaven with patience. Were it not
                            Some comfort to reflect your son has fallen
                            Fighting his country's cause? and for yourself
                            You will not in unpitied poverty
                            Be left to mourn his loss. Your grateful country
                            Amid the triumph of her victory

Remember those who paid its price of blood,
And with a noble charity relieves
The widow and the orphan.

WOMAN.
    God reward them!
God bless them, it will help me in my age
But Sir! it will not pay me for my child!

TRAVELLER.
  Was he your only child?

WOMAN.
     My only one,
The stay and comfort of my widowhood,
A dear good boy!--when first he went to sea
I felt what it would come to,--something told me
I should be childless soon. But tell me Sir
If it be true that for a hurt like his
There is no cure? please God to spare his life
Tho' he be blind, yet I should be so thankful!
I can remember there was a blind man
Lived in our village, one from his youth up
Quite dark, and yet he was a merry man,
And he had none to tend on him so well
As I would tend my boy!

TRAVELLER.
  Of this be sure
His hurts are look'd to well, and the best help
The place affords, as rightly is his due,
Ever at hand. How happened it he left you?
Was a seafaring life his early choice?

WOMAN.
  No Sir! poor fellow--he was wise enough
To be content at home, and 'twas a home
As comfortable Sir I even tho' I say it,
As any in the country. He was left
A little boy when his poor father died,

Just old enough to totter by himself
And call his mother's name. We two were all,
And as we were not left quite destitute
We bore up well. In the summer time I worked
Sometimes a-field. Then I was famed for knitting,
And in long winter nights my spinning wheel
Seldom stood still. We had kind neighbours too
And never felt distress. So he grew up
A comely lad and wonderous well disposed;
I taught him well; there was not in the parish
A child who said his prayers more regular,
Or answered readier thro' his catechism.
If I had foreseen this! but 'tis a blessing
We do'nt know what we're born to!

TRAVELLER.
        But how came it
He chose to be a Sailor?

WOMAN.
        You shall hear Sir;
As he grew up he used to watch the birds
In the corn, child's work you know, and easily done.
'Tis an idle sort of task, so he built up
A little hut of wicker-work and clay
Under the hedge, to shelter him in rain.
And then he took for very idleness
To making traps to catch the plunderers,
All sorts of cunning traps that boys can make--
Propping a stone to fall and shut them in,
Or crush them with its weight, or else a springe
Swung on a bough. He made them cleverly--
And I, poor foolish woman! I was pleased
To see the boy so handy. You may guess
What followed Sir from this unlucky skill.
He did what he should not when he was older:
I warn'd him oft enough; but he was caught
In wiring hares at last, and had his choice
The prison or the ship.

TRAVELLER.
    The choice at least

Was kindly left him, and for broken laws
This was methinks no heavy punishment.

WOMAN.
So I was told Sir. And I tried to think so,
But 'twas a sad blow to me! I was used
To sleep at nights soundly and undisturb'd--
Now if the wind blew rough, it made me start
And think of my poor boy tossing about
Upon the roaring seas. And then I seem'd
To feel that it was hard to take him from me
For such a little fault. But he was wrong
Oh very wrong--a murrain on his traps!
See what they've brought him too!

TRAVELLER.
Well! well! take comfort
He will be taken care of if he lives;
And should you lose your child, this is a country
Where the brave sailor never leaves a parent
To weep for him in want.

WOMAN.
Sir I shall want
No succour long. In the common course of years
I soon must be at rest, and 'tis a comfort
When grief is hard upon me to reflect
It only leads me to that rest the sooner.

1: The stink-pots used on board the French ships. In the engagement between the Mars and L'Hercule, some of our sailors were shockingly mangled by them: One in particular, as described in the Eclogue, lost both his eyes. It would be policy and humanity to employ means of destruction, could they be discovered, powerful enough todestroy fleets and armies, but to use any thing that only inflicts additional torture upon the victims of our war systems, is cruel andwicked.

ECLOGUE V

THE WITCH

NATHANIEL.
>Father! here father! I have found a horse-shoe!
>Faith it was just in time, for t'other night
>I laid two straws across at Margery's door,
>And afterwards I fear'd that she might do me
>A mischief for't. There was the Miller's boy
>Who set his dog at that black cat of hers,
>I met him upon crutches, and he told me
>'Twas all her evil eye.

FATHER.
>>'Tis rare good luck;
>I would have gladly given a crown for one
>If t'would have done as well. But where did'st find it?

NATHANIEL.
>Down on the Common; I was going a-field
>And neighbour Saunders pass'd me on his mare;
>He had hardly said "good day," before I saw
>The shoe drop off; 'twas just upon my tongue
>To call him back,--it makes no difference, does it.
>Because I know whose 'twas?

FATHER.
>>Why no, it can't.
>The shoe's the same you know, and you 'did find' it.

NATHANIEL.
>That mare of his has got a plaguey road
>To travel, father, and if he should lame her,
>For she is but tender-footed,--

FATHER.
>>Aye, indeed--
>I should not like to see her limping back
>Poor beast! but charity begins at home,

    And Nat, there's our own horse in such a way
    This morning!

NATHANIEL.
        Why he ha'nt been rid again!
    Last night I hung a pebble by the manger
    With a hole thro', and every body says
    That 'tis a special charm against the hags.

FATHER.
    It could not be a proper natural hole then,
    Or 'twas not a right pebble,--for I found him
    Smoking with sweat, quaking in every limb,
    And panting so! God knows where he had been
    When we were all asleep, thro' bush and brake
    Up-hill and down-hill all alike, full stretch
    At such a deadly rate!--

NATHANIEL.
        By land and water,
    Over the sea perhaps!--I have heard tell
    That 'tis some thousand miles, almost at the end
    Of the world, where witches go to meet the Devil.
    They used to ride on broomsticks, and to smear
    Some ointment over them and then away
    Out of the window! but 'tis worse than all
    To worry the poor beasts so. Shame upon it
    That in a Christian country they should let
    Such creatures live!

FATHER.
        And when there's such plain proof!
    I did but threaten her because she robb'd
    Our hedge, and the next night there came a wind
    That made me shake to hear it in my bed!
    How came it that that storm unroofed my barn,
    And only mine in the parish? look at her
    And that's enough; she has it in her face--
    A pair of large dead eyes, rank in her head,
    Just like a corpse, and purs'd with wrinkles round,
    A nose and chin that scarce leave room between

For her lean fingers to squeeze in the snuff,
And when she speaks! I'd sooner hear a raven
Croak at my door! she sits there, nose and knees
Smoak-dried and shrivell'd over a starved fire,
With that black cat beside her, whose great eyes
Shine like old Beelzebub's, and to be sure
It must be one of his imps!--aye, nail it hard.

NATHANIEL.
    I wish old Margery heard the hammer go!
    She'd curse the music.

FATHER.
        Here's the Curate coming,
    He ought to rid the parish of such vermin;
    In the old times they used to hunt them out
    And hang them without mercy, but Lord bless us!
    The world is grown so wicked!

CURATE.
        Good day Farmer!
    Nathaniel what art nailing to the threshold?

NATHANIEL.
    A horse-shoe Sir, 'tis good to keep off witchcraft,
    And we're afraid of Margery.

CURATE.
        Poor old woman!
    What can you fear from her?

FATHER.
        What can we fear?
    Who lamed the Miller's boy? who rais'd the wind
    That blew my old barn's roof down? who d'ye think
    Rides my poor horse a'nights? who mocks the hounds?
    But let me catch her at that trick again,
    And I've a silver bullet ready for her,
    One that shall lame her, double how she will.

NATHANIEL.
>What makes her sit there moping by herself,
>With no soul near her but that great black cat?
>And do but look at her!

CURATE.
>   Poor wretch! half blind
>And crooked with her years, without a child
>Or friend in her old age, 'tis hard indeed
>To have her very miseries made her crimes!
>I met her but last week in that hard frost
>That made my young limbs ache, and when I ask'd
>What brought her out in the snow, the poor old woman
>Told me that she was forced to crawl abroad
>And pick the hedges, just to keep herself
>From perishing with cold, because no neighbour
>Had pity on her age; and then she cried,
>And said the children pelted her with snow-balls,
>And wish'd that she were dead.

FATHER.
>   I wish she was!
>She has plagued the parish long enough!

CURATE.
>   Shame farmer!
>Is that the charity your bible teaches?

FATHER.
>My bible does not teach me to love witches.
>I know what's charity; who pays his tithes
>And poor-rates readier?

CURATE.
>   Who can better do it?
>You've been a prudent and industrious man,
>And God has blest your labour.

FATHER.
>   Why, thank God Sir,

I've had no reason to complain of fortune.

CURATE.
    Complain! why you are wealthy. All the parish
    Look up to you.

FATHER.
        Perhaps Sir, I could tell
    Guinea for guinea with the warmest of them.

CURATE.
    You can afford a little to the poor,
    And then what's better still, you have the heart
    To give from your abundance.

FATHER.
          God forbid
    I should want charity!

CURATE.
        Oh! 'tis a comfort
    To think at last of riches well employ'd!
    I have been by a death-bed, and know the worth
    Of a good deed at that most awful hour
    When riches profit not.
          Farmer, I'm going
    To visit Margery. She is sick I hear--
    Old, poor, and sick! a miserable lot,
    And death will be a blessing. You might send her
    Some little matter, something comfortable,
    That she may go down easier to the grave
    And bless you when she dies.

FATHER.
        What! is she going!
    Well God forgive her then! if she has dealt
    In the black art. I'll tell my dame of it,
    And she shall send her something.

CURATE.
>So I'll say;
>And take my thanks for her's. ['goes']

FATHER.
>That's a good man
>That Curate, Nat, of ours, to go and visit
>The poor in sickness; but he don't believe
>In witchcraft, and that is not like a christian.

NATHANIEL.
>And so old Margery's dying!

FATHER.
>But you know
>She may recover; so drive t'other nail in!

ECLOGUE VI

THE RUINED COTTAGE

Aye Charles! I knew that this would fix thine eye,
This woodbine wreathing round the broken porch,
Its leaves just withering, yet one autumn flower
Still fresh and fragrant; and yon holly-hock
That thro' the creeping weeds and nettles tall
Peers taller, and uplifts its column'd stem
Bright with the broad rose-blossoms. I have seen
Many a fallen convent reverend in decay,
And many a time have trod the castle courts
And grass-green halls, yet never did they strike
Home to the heart such melancholy thoughts
As this poor cottage. Look, its little hatch
Fleeced with that grey and wintry moss; the roof
Part mouldered in, the rest o'ergrown with weeds,
House-leek and long thin grass and greener moss;
So Nature wars with all the works of man.
And, like himself, reduces back to earth
His perishable piles.
              I led thee here
Charles, not without design; for this hath been
My favourite walk even since I was a boy;
And I remember Charles, this ruin here,
The neatest comfortable dwelling place!
That when I read in those dear books that first
Woke in my heart the love of poesy,
How with the villagers Erminia dwelt,
And Calidore for a fair shepherdess
Forgot his quest to learn the shepherd's lore;
My fancy drew from, this the little hut
Where that poor princess wept her hopeless love,
Or where the gentle Calidore at eve
Led Pastorella home. There was not then
A weed where all these nettles overtop
The garden wall; but sweet-briar, scenting sweet
The morning air, rosemary and marjoram,
All wholesome herbs; and then, that woodbine wreath'd
So lavishly around the pillared porch
Its fragrant flowers, that when I past this way,
After a truant absence hastening home,
I could not chuse but pass with slacken'd speed
By that delightful fragrance. Sadly changed

Is this poor cottage! and its dwellers, Charles!--
Theirs is a simple melancholy tale,
There's scarce a village but can fellow it,
And yet methinks it will not weary thee,
And should not be untold.
              A widow woman
Dwelt with her daughter here; just above want,
She lived on some small pittance that sufficed,
In better times, the needful calls of life,
Not without comfort. I remember her
Sitting at evening in that open door way
And spinning in the sun; methinks I see her
Raising her eyes and dark-rimm'd spectacles
To see the passer by, yet ceasing not
To twirl her lengthening thread. Or in the garden
On some dry summer evening, walking round
To view her flowers, and pointing, as she lean'd
Upon the ivory handle of her stick,
To some carnation whose o'erheavy head
Needed support, while with the watering-pot
Joanna followed, and refresh'd and trimm'd
The drooping plant; Joanna, her dear child,
As lovely and as happy then as youth
And innocence could make her.
                  Charles! it seems
As tho' I were a boy again, and all
The mediate years with their vicissitudes
A half-forgotten dream. I see the Maid
So comely in her Sunday dress! her hair,
Her bright brown hair, wreath'd in contracting curls,
And then her cheek! it was a red and white
That made the delicate hues of art look loathsome,
The countrymen who on their way to church
Were leaning o'er the bridge, loitering to hear
The bell's last summons, and in idleness
Watching the stream below, would all look up
When she pass'd by. And her old Mother, Charles!
When I have heard some erring infidel
Speak of our faith as of a gloomy creed,
Inspiring fear and boding wretchedness.
Her figure has recurr'd; for she did love
The sabbath-day, and many a time has cross'd
These fields in rain and thro' the winter snows.
When I, a graceless boy, wishing myself
By the fire-side, have wondered why 'she' came

Who might have sate at home.
                One only care
Hung on her aged spirit. For herself,
Her path was plain before her, and the close
Of her long journey near. But then her child
Soon to be left alone in this bad world,--
That was a thought that many a winter night
Had kept her sleepless: and when prudent love
In something better than a servant's slate
Had placed her well at last, it was a pang
Like parting life to part with her dear girl.

One summer, Charles, when at the holydays
Return'd from school, I visited again
My old accustomed walks, and found in them.
A joy almost like meeting an old friend,
I saw the cottage empty, and the weeds
Already crowding the neglected flowers.
Joanna by a villain's wiles seduced
Had played the wanton, and that blow had reach'd
Her mother's heart. She did not suffer long,
Her age was feeble, and the heavy blow
Brought her grey hairs with sorrow to the grave.

I pass this ruin'd dwelling oftentimes
And think of other days. It wakes in me
A transient sadness, but the feelings Charles
That ever with these recollections rise,
I trust in God they will not pass away.

                                              THE END

Echo Library
www.echo-library.com

Echo Library uses advanced digital print-on-demand technology to build and preserve an exciting world class collection of rare and out-of-print books, making them readily available for everyone to enjoy.

Situated just yards from Teddington Lock on the River Thames, Echo Library was founded in 2005 by Tom Cherrington, a specialist dealer in rare and antiquarian books with a passion for literature.

Please visit our website for a complete catalogue of our books, which includes foreign language titles.

The Right to Read

Echo Library actively supports the Royal National Institute for the Blind's Right to Read initiative by publishing a comprehensive range of Large Print (16 point Tiresias font as recommended by the RNIB) and Clear Print (14 point Tiresias font) titles for those who find standard print difficult to read.

Customer Service

If there is a serious error in the text or layout please send details to feedback@echo-library.com and we will supply a corrected copy. If there is a printing fault or the book is damaged please refer to your supplier.

Printed in the United Kingdom
by Lightning Source UK Ltd.
127535UK00002B/305/A